ENCOUNTERS
WITH
ISRAELI
AUTHORS

esther fuchs

micah publications

Encounters With Israeli Authors Copyright © 1982
by Esther Fuchs

Typeset by Roberta Kalechofsky
Cover Design: Robert and Roberta Kalechofsky
Production and Technical Assistance: Robert Kalechofsky
Printed by McNaughton & Gunn, Ann Arbor, Michigan 48106

Cataloguing in Publication Data: Bibliography: p.
1. Authors, Israeli--Interviews. 2. Israeli literature--
History and Criticism--Addresses, essays, lectures.
I. Fuchs, Esther, 1953-
PJ5021.E52   1983   892.4'6'09   82-62086
ISBN: 0-916288-14-5 Allen County Public Library
                      Ft. Wayne, Indiana

Acknowledgements:
Interview with Aharon Appelfeld was originally published in
Genesis 2, June 1978.
Interview with Amalia Kahana-Carmon was originally
published in Modern Hebrew Literature, Vol. 6, no.3-4,
1981.

MICAH PUBLICATIONS
255 Humphrey Street
Marblehead, Massachusetts
01945

TABLE OF CONTENTS

mp

YEHUDA AMICHAI and ESTHER FUCHS

INTRODUCTION

The literary enterprise in which Israeli writers are engaged is unique. In addition to the writer's usual struggle with words, the Israeli writer must continue to create a language as he creates a fictional literary situation. In the words of Aharon Megged, "Hebrew is not yet used enough"; like a new garment it is somewhat stiff. Having become a spoken language only in the 20th century, it does not yet afford the writer with good models for dialogue, for example. The resurrection of the ancient Biblical language and its adaptation to modern life still continues, with new expressions and phrases created by the Hebrew Language Academy. Since the Hebrew language has evolved as a nonsacral fictional medium only in the last two hundred years, the Hebrew literary tradition does not provide the contemporary author with accessible or stable models. The language is evolving so rapidly, that even the literary styles of authors who wrote in the 1930s and 1940s seems antiquated and quaint. Finally, many Israeli authors (e.g. Aharon Appelfeld and Itamar Yaoz-Kest) are immigrants, whose mother tongue is not Hebrew, and for whom each writing experience is a renewed struggle not only with a new language but with a new culture.

The volatile political situation of Israel, a country that has survived four major wars since its establishment in 1948, creates additional pressures for the Israeli writer, not only because of the traditional enmity between canons and muses, but because of the social significance of the writer's occupation in Jewish tradition. As Yoram Kaniuk says, "Who were the prophets, after all? They were the poets of antiquity."

Since its inception in the 18th century, modern Hebrew literature has been inextricably intertwined with the national history, reflecting its dramatic vicissitudes and endorsing or criticising its major developments. Israeli writers are still expected to give precedence to national subjects, and arguments concerning the writer's social duties and national responsibilities still continue in Israeli literary forums.

Israel's economic constraints do not help its writers either. Most writers work in full-time jobs in addition to their creative activities. Even the most celebrated authors are compelled to find gainful employment to make ends meet. As A. B. Yehoshua stated, "Here, in Israel. . .writing is an ideal, a vocation, a social responsibility, a goal in life. When it becomes a lucrative business too, it's confusing. . . ."

The present collection of interviews introduces, among other things, the problems, frustrations, hopes and rewards shared by contemporary Israeli writers. It is an outgrowth of an article written in 1977, "To Be or Not to Be an Israeli Writer Today," in which I discussed the logic and paradoxes of contemporary Israeli literature from the author's point of view. In my striving for authenticity, I turned to the writers themselves, asking them to define their own point of view in their own words. One question led to another and one interview paved the way for the next. The month I intended to dedicate to the article grew into a five year span of periodical shuttles to Israel and back. The writer's point of view of Israeli literature and his self perception as Israeli writer continue to be prevailing themes in the present collection. However, in addition to these issues, the interviews focus on the specific works of each writer, his treatment of theme and his personal style as well as his views on criticism, writing and art in general.

All the writers included in this volume are highly respected, widely read and well known in Israel, yet they constitute only part of the major writers of the country. Since they are representative of the major trends in contemporary Israeli fiction, this collection ought to be considered as a paradigmatic rather than comprehensive sample of Israeli writers. Each one of these writers offers a representative and, at the same time, intensely personal view of the Israeli literary scene. They rarely agree with each other about the aims, goals, achievements and problems of contemporary Hebrew literature, yet they are equally adamant about their respective views.

In writing these interviews, I tried to recreate the sense of surprise I experienced throughout my encounters with the writers. These encounters challenged my preconceived notions about these writers--notions based on my acquaintance with their works and their critical appraisal. Writers known for their social commitment and political involvement unexpectedly emphasized the aesthetic and personal aspects of their work, while those who had won recognition for their universal allegories expatiated on the importance of national culture; and native writers whose interest in Judaism seemed not to be significant, insisted precisely on that interest.

As a literary critic, I had been trained to avoid consulting writers when analysing or evaluating their work. It seems to me, however, that the critical transgression I committed was worth the effort because the writers' "intentional fallacies" taught me more about their literary creativity than many a critical essay. The subjective perspective of the writers compelled me to reassess the validity of "objective criticism" and dramatized for me the restrictive scope of criticism divorced from life. The author may not be the best judge of his own work, but he is the final authority on his desires, memories, illusions and disappointments--the stuff that his literature is, in the final analysis, made of. By the same token, the interview format, which catches the writer offguard and forces him to be spontaneous, may not serve as conclusive proof in a critical context, but it is an invaluable source for learning about the person behind the literary persona, the living presence behind the printed page.

Some writers made my work easier, responding with gusto, volubility and eloquence. Others were reticent and economical, forcing me to content myself with the questions they were willing to address themselves to. I made an effort to present the writers as interlocutors and, above all, as individual personalities, not only by reporting their words, but by reproducing the way in which they expressed themselves. To my regret, much of the original flavor had to be sacrificed through the process of translation. Nevertheless, I feel that I succeeded in communicating at least my own curiosity and excitement as interviewer, and the frankness and earnestness with which the interviewees responded.

The discussion with the Israeli critic, Gershon Shaked, serves as a general introduction to the state of Israeli letters. The interviews are arranged in order to enhance their mutual incongruity rather than by the chronological order in which they were undertaken. Most of the interviews were conducted in Israel, during the period 1977-1982, with the exception of that with Yehuda Amichai, which began in Jerusalem, August 1981, and was completed in Austin, Texas, March, 1982. The interview with Amalia Kahana-Carmon was published in <u>Modern Hebrew Literature</u> in Spring, 1980 the interview with A. B. Yehoshua will be published in Midstream magazine.

I wish to thank all the distinguished writers for their cooperation, candidness and willingness to share their time and thoughts with me. I thank Roberta Kalechofsky for her useful comments and editorial help and, above all, her genuine interest in this project. I also wish to acknowledge the technical help and moral support of Zila and David Fuks and Noel Wolf.

Esther Fuchs
Austin, Texas
Sept., 1982

GERSHON SHAKED

Gershon Shaked, scholar and critic of modern Hebrew literature, was born in Vienna in 1929, and emigrated to Israel in 1939. He graduated from Herzeliah High School in 1948, and continued his studies at Hebrew University, receiving his B. A. in 1954, and his Ph. D. in 1964. He did post graduate work at the University of Zurich from 1964 to 1965, and taught at Hebrew University from 1962-1967. From 1968-1970 he was chairman of the Department of Theatrical Arts at Tel Aviv University; and since 1973 he has been professor of Hebrew literature and the chairman of the Department of Hebrew Literature at Hebrew University. He was visiting professor at Hebrew Union College from 1968 to 1969, and at Harvard University in 1975.

Among his publications are: Arba'ah Sipurim (four stories, on the theory of prose fiction) 1963; Bekhi va-dema (Laughter and Tears--The works of Mendele Mokher Sefarim) 1964; The Hebrew Historical Drama in the 20th Century, 1970; Gal hadash ba-siporet ha-ivrit (A New Wave in Hebrew Fiction) 1971; Im Tishkah ei pa'am (If You Ever Forget: On Jewish American fiction) 1972; Omanut ha-sipur shel shai agnon (The Narrative Art of S. Y. Agnon) 1973; Lelo motsa (Dead End--on the works of J. S. Brenner and his contemporaries) 1973; Bialik-yetsirato lesugeha bi-rei (The genres of Bialik's works as reflected in criticism) 1974; Hasiporet ha-ivrit 1880-1970 (Hebrew fiction 1880-1970) 1977.

Is Israeli Literature Jewish?

An Interview with Gershon Shaked*

E. F. Some critics maintain that the great Israeli novel has not yet been written. Do you agree?

G. S. I am not sure I understand what they mean by "great." If these critics judge by the norms of the 19th century novelistic tradition, they might be right. By these norms, S. Yizhar's momentous Days of Ziklag is not a novel at all, because it does not offer a conventional plot progression. Yizhar is unique even among twentieth century writers. His sensitivity to mood and scenery and his attention to the most minute details can hardly be paralleled by Western novelists, perhaps with the exception of Thomas Wolfe.

E. F. Several authors I interviewed agreed that the quality of Israeli poetry is both quantitatively and qualitatively stronger than Israeli prose fiction.

G. S. You know, if the Nobel Prize were to be distributed to a nation as a whole, the Jews would receive it. Not for their contributions in physics, medicine or literature, but for their remarkable talent for self criticism. A good number of novels and novellas have been published in the last years. Tamuz, Megged, Bartov, Frenkel, Shahar, Orpaz, Yehoshua, Oz, Sadeh, Karmon, Kenaz write and continue to write, and I see no sign of fatigue. On the contrary. New and talented novelists are making a very pro-

* Jerusalem, August, 1977.

mising debut. I don't think they are in any sense inferior to our burgeoning poetry. If I were you I would not ask authors to judge their own works, especially if they happen to be Jewish.

E.F. Baruch Kurzweil criticized the writers you have mentioned for their superficiality and lack of historical perspective.

G.S. Kurzweil's literary criticism is based on his historiosophy. According to him, Zionism broke with Judaism, and consequently it has no chance or right to survive, not even as a culture. With such an approach, it is easy to find reasons which would deny the value of specific works. Controversies over the nature of modern Hebrew literature in Palestine started in the beginning of the twentieth century. Some argued that it should reflect life in the motherland, in the new space, others argued that it ought to continue the Jewish tradition, in time. The first argued that the new literature had to focus on the Middle Eastern experience, while their opponents claimed that it had been forged in Europe. Kurzweil belongs to the second camp. His underlying idea is that Zionism is radical change, and change is by definition destructive. Therefore, any literary innovation in Israeli writing is suspect. Kurzweil judges Israeli fiction by the critical standards of German Romanticism. In Kurzweil's opinion, Yizhar's mode of characterization is poor because the characters are not the individualized figures of Hesse, and they are not alienated from their society like those of Musil and Broch. Yizhar's characters are monochromatic because they symbolize different aspects of a collective experience. Yizhar tried to repossess the land through words. And his verbal possession of space is also related to historical roots. "Ziklag" is after all a Biblical city. If you are willing to accept the literary legitimacy of the collective experience, Days of Ziklag is an

3

artistic tour de force that any national literature should be proud of.

E. F. What do you think of Eli Shweid's thesis concerning the "Sorrow of the Severed Roots?"

G. S. Shweid follows in fact Kurzweil's point of view. The "severed roots" hypothesis is very one-sided. After all, Israeli literature is not much more severed than the Hebrew literature which was produced in the diaspora, which synthesized Jewish and European values. In the nineteen twenties, Palestinian literature reduced its indebtedness to the Jewish as well as to the European literary tradition. In the thirties and forties, the Western influence increased and reached its peak in the fifties and sixties. Yet, the dialectical relationship between immanent and external forces continues. It is true that most contemporary authors did not go to Yeshiva. But most of them browsed through Bialik and Ravnizki's Anthology of Rabbinic Stories. Even in the present secular society, every Jewish child absorbs the cycle of Jewish holidays. It becomes part of his life's rhythm, just as in a traditional society. These are roots. Solidarity and mutual responsibility in the Israeli army, the loyalty and the love for the country, these too are roots. But by the same token, Mendele didn't know what life in a Jewish land means.

E. F. You see Israeli literature as both a rebellion against and a continuation of Jewish tradition?

G. S. In cultural and literary history things cannot get lost. They only become transformed. The Zionist antithesis contains the Jewish antithesis. So does Israeli literature. Take Amos Oz's Unto Death, for example. It is very close to The Tribe of Judah by di Verga. One can easily detect the fear and anguish of the persecuted Jew. It evokes the most authentic characteristics of Jewish martyrology. This

4

is the central theme of Aharon Appelfeld. In poetry, the dialectical relationship with the Jewish sources is even more obtrusive. Yehudah Amichai uses Biblical and liturgical elements constantly. He may use them parodically, still, the connection is there.

E. F.   What about contemporary fiction written by Jewish American authors. What are the Jewish characteristics of this literature?

G. S.   In my book, If You Ever Forget, I examine the similarities between contemporary American Jewish literature and German Jewish literature between the two wars. In both literatures Jewish writers offer the most intense expression to the cultural and social predicament of the intellectual in modern society. These authors focus on the isolation and alienation of the individual in the modern mass society. The most frequent protagonists in both Jewish literary contexts are exiles: Bellow's Sammler and Herzog are not very different from Wasserman's Caspar Hauser or Kafka's Joseph K. There are also interesting analogies between Agnon's Tziril in A Simple Story and Philip Roth's castrating yiddishe mamas, in Goodbye Columbus and Portnoy's Complaint. The interesting thing is that Yehoshua and Amos Oz continue to reflect a similar sense of exile, alienation, contrary to our expectations from Sabra writers. George Friedman wrote in his Fin du Peuple Juif, that Jewish literature came to an end because it no longer depicts the Jewish angoisse. But the fear and anguish of a weak and isolated minority in the midst of a hostile and uncomprehending world pervades Bellow and Malamud as well as Oz and Yehoshua. In this sense, the insouciant buoyance of Moshe Shamir, and to an extent of S. Yizhar is nothing but an episode in the history of modern Hebrew literature.

5

E. F. Is a sense of alienation enough to make up for the loss of Jewish traditional values--as a fictional theme?

G. S. It is true that Jewish halacha ceased to perform the central function it did before the twentieth cnetury. But it did not disappear either. The ideal of halacha was transformed by modern Zionism into the ideal of hagshama. *
Socialist Zionists interpreted religious observance into human-socialist activism. In America, the tradition of Jewish mutual responsibility continues in the form of the communal institutions of welfare. When Bialik said, "give us mitzvot," he didn't mean religious observances, but social responsibilities. The concept of "to be or not to be" is a misrepresentation of modern Jewish reality. We must understand, that even when we don't observe religious laws, we observe Judaism in different ways. This consciousness is crucial for our survival as Jews both in Israel and in the United States.

* to realize an idea or theory in the practice of it

———— *gs* ————

AMALIA KAHANA-CARMON

Amalia Kahana-Carmon was born in kibbutz Ein Harod. She studied at Herzeliah High School in Tel Aviv and later majored in the Hebrew language, Hebrew literature, and Biblical studies at Hebrew University. Kahana-Carmon worked as the secretary of the educational department of the Zionist Federation in Britain and as secretary of the Israeli consulate in London. An academic librarian by profession, she worked at the central library of Tel Aviv University in 1963-1965. She has been writer-in-residence at Tel Aviv University. In addition to her literary writing, she has published several critical essays. Her first book, Bi-Khefifah Ahat (Under One Roof) is a collection of short stories published in 1966. This was followed by Ve-Yareah-be-emek ayalon (Moon in the Valley of Ajalon) published in 1971, and Sadot Magnetiim: triptikhon (Magnetic Fields: A Triptych), 1977.

We Are All Magnetic Fields

An Interview with Amalia Kahana-Carmon*

Amalia Kahana-Carmon is often described as the Israeli Virginia Woolf. Though she belongs to the age group of the Palmach generation of the fifties, she is normally classified as one of the "New Wave" writers on a par with A. B. Yehoshua and Amos Oz.

E. F. What do you think of the way in which you are described?

A. K. -C. What do these names contribute? Each author has a unique style, all his own. However, if it makes it easier for those who don't read me in the original to understand me better, all right, let it be. Still, I believe every author is unique and every work is too, due to its unique style.

E. F. Could you define or describe your own style?

A. K. -C. Style is a part and parcel of the expression. I never "think out" devices. The device is a reflection of my psychic structure. It's like my own voice. Part of it is the sound, the other part--my intonation. (She stops. She is not one to wander off into audible musings, which are the interviewer's delight. I can detect the familiar excruciatingly meticulous care in her speech as well. She will not add a single word if it is unnecessary.)

* Tel Aviv, August, 1977.

8

E. F.   Could you tell me more about literature as an expression, and what your writing means to you?

A. K. -C.   A writer is a person who at a certain point in his life has found out that he is bothered by something which those around him seem to take in their stride.   He finds out that here the usual modes of talk will not do, and he turns to investigate it the lonely way--on paper.   It is doubtful if he is to find a solution to those pestering questions, but giving shape to his probings is itself a kind of solace.   And then, something strange happens.   The paper gets hold of him.   It stimulates him, it becomes a meaning to itself. This person has passed a thin line into a new, a different world, to stay there forever.   Forever, because not to obey this call now is tantamount to desertion, or still worse, to exile.

E. F.   What are the questions which obsess you?   What do you write about?

A. K. -C.   I must give you a short answer at the risk of making a silly reduction, but I can't help it, I cannot do justice to your question, but I have no choice.   (Pause)   I think I am mostly concerned with two issues: death-in-life versus life, and chaos versus order.   These two are clearly intertwined, of course.   I am talking about the individual revolt against the established order of things, the attempt to break through the visible.   This attempt brings about an epiphany of a wider order of things which underlies our existence.

E. F.   I am not sure I understand.

A. K. -C.   Every story is a breakthrough.   Every story is catching a glimpse of some vast, infinite pattern which gives meaning to our lives.   Every story is an acceptance, a realization that the all-encompassing pattern is there for a purpose.   But the unconscious attempt to disguise the

9

pattern is infinite, so every story comes as a surprise.

E. F. You tend to use religious terminology when describing your artistic experience. Are you aware of such elements in your writing?

A. K. -C. Religious in the universal sense, yes, maybe. If you mean religious in the Jewish sense—there may be some such element in my writing. My work is an expression of myself, and I happen to be Jewish, I guess my point of view is affected by a hierarchy of values which is bound up with this point in history, and this place in the world. And I guess there is no escape from my own point of view. In other words, consciously I am trying to tell of what I perceive to be a universal truth.

E. F. How does the fact that you live in Israel now, a state in constant strife, affect your writing?

A. K. -C. Being too close to things, I wouldn't know. Just as one couldn't answer whether the knowledge that we are prone to the common cold, or to cancer, affects our daily lives. I have two sons in the military service, one in the Air Force and one in the Army. So nobody can be against war more than myself. But to tell the truth, during the day to day routine, doing the normal things, small or great, war hardly enters our thoughts. It becomes a fact of life. Almost like air pollution. I have come to realize that the daily routine, the way we live the simple moments in our lives, is by far more important, more decisive, more meaningful to me, and I think to many others as well.

E. F. You have recently published a novel, a triptych to be precise, entitled <u>Magnetic Fields</u>. Could you tell me what are these magnetic fields?

10

A.K.-C. Every human encounter is the external embodiment of an attraction between two magnetic fields. The encounter comes suddenly, unexpectedly. It is a moment of truth. It is a moment of revelation, as when the right ray of sun penetrates through the right window pane, and falls with the right slant on one picture in the museum. This is the painfully short moment which shows us just what the artist had in mind. It happened to me once. I walked into a bookstore in Jerusalem. I opened one book after another, when suddenly I found myself reading something breathlessly. It was a book of poems by Pinhas Sadeh. There was a flash, I was touched by something powerful. For some reason, I could not purchase the book right away. A while later, back in Tel Aviv, I went to buy the book. When I opened it this time it was--- difficult. The angle had changed. The ray of light passed me by. There was no illumination. The same happens with human encounters. We meet someone, and suddenly we are capable of being ourselves, just like we were supposed to be--ourselves without hiding, without pretending, with no pretexts. We are each a magnetic field. And each attraction, limited as it may appear to be, is a cosmic happening--it occurs within the broader pattern of things, within the endlessly complex structure which under-lies our lives.

E.F. In "There, The Newsroom" you use a man as your first person protagonist-narrator. Is there a difference between the way men and women in your stories perceive or react to relationships?

A.K.-C. First, I hope Zevulun Leipzig is authentic. I had my intuition alone to rely on, no personal experience. But, to answer your question, I don't think there is a significant difference or rather essential difference between men and women in this regard. What I am depicting is a human condition which is not contingent on gender. Of course men attract or are attracted in a different way, but that is not of the essence.

E. F. What does the title of the story, "There, The Newsroom" mean?

A. K. -C. The essential news, the news which matters, is not in the newsroom but in the opposite direction. The things which shape our lives are not projected on the television screen.

E. F. It seems to me that the dynamics of human encounters is a predominant theme in your earlier writings as well. Your first collection of short stories, Under One Roof, and your novel, And Moon in the Valley of Ajallon, portray encounters which are doomed to failure.

A. K. -C. This is my understanding of human encounters in general. Living in a world of flux, subjugated to the indecipherable laws of constant vicissitudes, our encounters cannot but be momentary flashes. The glamor cannot last because we change, the others change, circumstances change. So I wouldn't call the end of a relationship a failure. (Smiling) You mention my earlier writings. I, as a writer, have changed too. In my novel I think I was trying to depict the unyielding attempt to remain at the top. I don't mean "top" in the social sense. I'm referring to the emotional climax. I wrote about the hard way in which one learns the pain of the break between dream and reality. And you know, in the beginning I tended to write, for lack of a better term, in the "romantic" vein. I was trying to search for human nature through the external order of things. I wanted to touch human misery without getting my hands dirty, out of a peculiar fastidiousness. I think I changed tremendously in this sense. I am not as much of an outsider anymore. I am more capable now of observing the pain, and being part of it at the same time. I have

12

learned to come to terms with the "concrete" and naked reality and not flinch from expressing it in a more direct fashion.

E. F.   What are you trying to achieve by expressing it? How do you hope to affect the reader?

A.K.-C.   I have no control over the reader.   The reader changes just as much as I do.   You may not respond to a certain passage which does not appeal to you any longer. Now you might relate better to another passage, incident or character.   After all, what are we trying to find in a book?---Ourselves.   A good book offers you yourself in a more articulate way.   Reading is actually plunging into one's own identity and, one hopes, emerging stronger than before.   You see, unconsciously, we are seeking to find an affirmation to our own world perception and set of values. Since these change as we grow up and develop, our response to books changes as well.   I don't believe there is an objective yardstick by which a book may be evaluated.   The "science" of literary criticism is an illusion--it is based on subjective impressions, and no one feels the sting more strongly than I, being a critic myself.   The only thing I hope to do in my books, is to open up the reader to a new awareness.   There is no logical or speculative message I intend to transmit.   The "message" belongs to the realm of intuition, imagination and emotional perception.   If I manage to make a reader sensitive to that special awareness which has inspired me to write, I consider myself a lucky writer.

E.F.   I guess the following question is unavoidable.   Could you divulge any secrets about the technical aspects of your writing?   Do you write daily, for instance?

A.K.-C.   (Interrupting me with a bitter laugh)   I wish--

13

daily---No, unfortunately, I can't afford to devote that much time to my writing. As a wife, a housewife, and mother of three children, I could not possibly turn my passion into a daily routine, or discipline. I write when I cannot hold back any longer. Call it an attack, an irresistible impulse. In a way, my writing has almost been clandestine. There was a constant feeling of guilt, and a continuous tension between my duties at home and my literary aspirations. But it seems to me that now, with two children in the army, I need not feel as guilty as before. (As if stung by a familiar duty-bound impulse, she glances at her watch. Another magnetic field must be neutralized for a while, before it is defined on paper.)

YIZHAR SMILANSKY

Yizhar Smilansky signs his work, S. Yizhar. He was born in Rehovoth in 1916 to a family of farmers. His uncle, Moshe Smilansky, is a well known writer in Israel, of short stories and romances.

Yizhar Smilansky graduated from the teachers' seminary and Hebrew University and has taught at many schools and high schools, as well as being politically active in the Mapai, the Israel Labor Party, and serving as a member of the Knesset. He is currently a lecturer in the Department of Education at Hebrew University and his present literary concerns are mostly with theory and criticism, which was the subject of his doctoral thesis as well as of the numerous critical essays he has published in recent years. Yizhar won the Brenner Prize for 1950, and the Israel Prize in 1959.

His first story, "Ephraim hozer la-aspeset" (Ephraim Goes Back to Alfalfa) appeared in 1938. It was followed by Be-fa'at ei negev (At The End of the Negev) in 1945; Hahursha ba-giv'ah (The Forest on the Hill) 1947; Sipur Hirbat Hiz'eh (The Story of Hirbet Hiz'ah) 1949; and Shayara shel hatsot, 1950 (Midnight Convoy and Other Stories, 1969)*. Yemei ziklag (The Days of Ziklag) 1958 (excerpts in English in The Jewish Quarterly, v.6, no.3-4), Sipurei mishor (Stories of the Plain) 1963. He is also the author of several childrens' books. "The Prisoner" is available in English in Joel Blocker's edition of Israeli Stories, 1962.

*Title and date inside brackets indicate a publication in English.

15

I HOPE MY WORK WILL BE ENJOYED BY READERS WHO DON'T KNOW WHAT ARABS AND JEWS ARE

An Interview with S. Yizhar
(Tel Aviv, August 1977)

E.F. Yizhar Smilansky, in your very famous story, "The Prisoner," you describe a specific incident narrated from a personal-subjective perspective; but, in point of fact, the story gives expression to a universal problem, the unavoidable clash between ethical ideals and national reality. Would you agree that the story about the helpless Arab captive who unsettles the Israeli soldier, is also about the conflict between the Jewish ethical heritage and the Israeli struggle for survival?

S.Y. What do you mean by "clash," "survival?" Can't you see what you are doing? You are using the language of the mind. Jewish or not Jewish, Israeli and so forth, who cares? Is that what my story is about? The Israeli War of Independence will soon become a long-forgotten history. What remains is the music. Don't destroy the music. You see, you have been victimized by the vulgar interpretations of those who call themselves teachers and critics. They never grow tired of bastardizing literature. They turn the sublime into the most banal, petty and pedestrian. The only meaningful statement about art is "I like it" or "I don't like it." That's it. No more.

E.F. "The Prisoner" is only one of your stories about the conflict between the individual and the collective.

S.Y. What isn't about the tension between individual and collective? From the story of Noah in Genesis to James

16

Joyce, everything is about this conflict. This is too wide a category, you can fit almost any literary work into this scheme. Why classify? Why define? Why limit the scope of the work, by labeling it as this or that?

E. F. The theme of the individual versus society is particularly significant in the context of contemporary Israeli literature because what characterized the Palmach generation of the late forties and early fifties was a solidarity with the collective. Your work is cited as a major breakthrough, because it has questioned ideas previously taken for granted, such as the moral validity of Zionism.

S. Y. I am not flattered. Retroactively, you may be right. Considering certain developments which took place later, one can construe my work as a breakthrough. But as I told you, I am not flattered. I really don't care what "The Prisoner" means in sociological terms. I don't want people to read my story because it is "important" for the understanding of certain trends in Israeli literature. I don't want doctoral students, literary historians, or academics to congratulate me. To me it's utterly meaningless. The only relevant criterion, in my opinion, is whether the story "connects" or doesn't. Only scholars pay attention to the dates and circumstances, and the particular context is which a work of art is written, and they are the worst readers. They turn literature into sociology, politics, ideology, psychology, and philosophy. The fact is that all these are projections. In reality, there is one story, and this story works, or doesn't work. It either communicates with the reader, or it doesn't. If you identify with characters, if you get excited by the plot, if you find yourself in it--then, it's a good story. Since the critics are the worst readers and they must say something, they cling to the surface, to the subject matter. Of course, authors who lived during the Palmach period are most likely to use their specific experiences, the local color, the circumstances of their context, just as a sculptor who lives by a marble mine is most likely to use marble as his material, rather than wood. But the material does not matter. Those who are interested in material and history should go to the wax museum in London, and there they will get the picture in which they are interested. There it is cold and organized and classified and dead. Tolstoi is alive today not because he belonged to such and such a generation, but because his works are still interesting. War and Peace isn't exciting because of Napoleon or Czarist Russia, but because it is art. When you listen to good music, you enjoy it. You don't try to figure out whether it is romantic or baroque. At the root of the unfortunate distortion of literature into history lies our educational system. At school they teach you not how to experience literature, but how to become blind and dead to it. They desensitize you to its vividness and vibrancy, its unique color and smell. They teach it retroactively through the prism of groups and categories and periods and classes. The truth is that every author is a solitary man. The work is written in a quiet room far away from the maddening crowds, far away from the news of his day. In fact, in order to write, he must resist his context, and rebel against it. There are people who won't even start talking to you unless they know your financial income, your social status, your family, the country you came from, the language you speak. Can all these details describe you, your essence, your unique personality? These people confuse external trivialities with the thing itself. They do it because they are afraid to know, or perhaps because they don't know how to deal with the thing itself. Critics create artificial constructs in order to make their discussions of works of art easier and more convenient. That doesn't mean they understand art.

E. F. Critics also try to give us some objective criteria

18

for appreciating art. Should the value of art be determined by one's personal taste?

S. Y. There are no objective norms for evaluating art. Every critic, sophisticated as he may be, is a product of private inclinations and personal predilections. At the same time, there is no purely subjective evaluation either. We all are part of a certain cultural milieu, we don't choose our mother tongue, our first impressions and values. Whether we know it or not, we are influenced by trends and vogues, and we mouth opinions we imbibe from the cultural atmosphere we live in. You can't create things ex nihilo. You can't invent your favorite clothes, you must select them. Their form and color are predetermined by what is fashionable, by someone else's ideas of what is appropriate and beautiful. So there is no purely subjective, or individual evaluation. By the same token, nothing is purely dictated by objective norms, without being tainted with a personal touch. There are of course people whose ego is so worn out by prevailing ideas, they don't even know what they themselves like, and select what everyone else does.

E. F. According to you, then, there is no point in either teaching or discussing literature.

S. Y. There is no point in it if we try to explain. The only thing teachers should do is help us hear the music and the rhythm, help us penetrate into the essence, see the soul. But they rarely do it. They usually stay on the iconographic level. In other words, on the level which deals with the matter, with the concrete--the sculptor's block, the chunk of wood. They very rarely grasp the formal level, which is a higher level of perception. You see, this is the way I see it. There is still a higher step, the symbolic one. But the real understanding lies in the mystical phase. This is the highest. And they never reach it. Never! This is what I mean by "soul." At this phase,

19

specific identities turn into tensions, content becomes a
sheer energy of attraction and repulsion, structures dis-
solve into rhythms of appeal and response. It is almost
like a dance between reader and author. How can I explain
it? You must feel it. If you don't, there is no point in
describing it. How can I describe it? You know, in the
Frick Collection in New York--have you ever been there?
There are these two little paintings by Vermeer. I could
watch them for hours. If I were ever to go to the States,
these pictures would not let me feel it was a waste of time.
They have the rhythm I am talking about. Does that make
sense to you? Did you ever experience yellow? Yes,
yellow. The color. Now, try to explain that to a blind
man.

E. F. How should a story be read?

S. Y. This is what I am involved with in these days at the
school of education in Hebrew University. It is rather
complex, and I can't give you all the details, but basically,
the right process of reading literature consists of four
major phases. The first level is the iconographic one. It
deals with the mimetic aspect of the work, its relationship
to our social, political or cultural reality. At this level
you treat the characters as people you have met, sometime,
somewhere. You ask why they do what they do, what they
say, whether they understand things, whether you like them
or not.

The second level is symbolic. Here you deal with characters and events as vehicles of symbolic meaning. The
iconographic elements become signs in a code, and the
reader's job is to decode them, in order to understand
what they signify. At this point you see that Ephraim, who
confronts the kibbutz authorities, is an alienated man,
facing his fate in life, refusing to resign himself to it.
Perceived on this level, Michaelangelo's David is not a
young and gorgeous lad, who posed for the artist in his

atelier, but a symbol for the new emancipation of the Renaissance man.

The third level is the aesthetic level, in which you seek the reciprocal relationships between the different elements of the work, as well as their relationship to the whole. You ask why the artist placed specific elements in a specific constellation, what is the impact produced by the form, and what is implied by it.

The fourth level, which I consider the truly relevant perspective for literature, is the level of response. Here, you deal, not with subjects, themes or even forms, but with the appeal of the work. Here you respond with the innermost part of your personality, a part which is not rational or logical. Here you contemplate the thing itself, and what matters is the quality of the relationship between you as "I" and the cosmos as "I." This is the unique experience of responding to art, establishing a dialogue with it, enjoying it.

On the third level we are still dealing with quantities, with cold in relation to hot, with the tensions between high and low, close and distant. On the fourth level, however, even the tensions disappear. You are dealing with purely abstract qualities. So, if you ask questions about the individual and society, Zionism and Palestinians, or history and ideology, in order to pave the way for a higher and more refined perception of the artistic work, then you are doing the right thing. If the subject matter undergoes a transformation in the course of reading, then, and only then, your effort is not wasted.

The fourth level of response combines the sensual, emotional and intellectual perceptions. Reading literature is an art. You must sharpen your sensibilities, you must learn the steps, in order to dance to the rhythm. Art has a special rhythm. Let me give you an example in which the same thing is told in two different ways, in poetry and in prose-history. In the Iliad, Homer describes an old man who, offended by his peers, leaves his camp, returns to

21

the sea, and there, on the shore, prays to the gods for
revenge. "Silently the man went out to the stormy sea,"
says Homer. You see the storm, you feel the man's pain.
You sense the tension between his silence and the sea's
agitation, yet you perceive that, at the same time, the
man's silence is just as tumultuous as the stormy sea.
Plato reports the same incident, but in a radically different
way. He simply reports that the old man, having been
offended, left his camp and went to pray to the gods. The
facts are the same, but in Plato's report, we miss the
sensual perception, the nuanced details of sensibility and
emotion, the movement of the moment. That's why his
report is not poetry, it's not art, it's history. In Homer's
description the details are symbolic. The man who leaves
his camp to go to the sea, leaves civilization and culture,
social mores and conventions, and turns to nature. There
is a clear juxtaposition between society and nature, and an
enactment of a protest against the limitations of mankind.
Against the background of the stormy sea, the tragedy of
one single, solitary man takes on cosmic proportions.
Plato--who, as you know, wanted to banish the poets from
his republic because, in his opinion, their activity was
futile--Plato is not interested in rhythm, in artistic expression, but in the fact.

E. F. When you first wrote "The Prisoner" or "Havakuk,"
what moved you to do it? Was it a will to elicit a certain
response from the reader, or spontaneous anger--a will
to protest?

S. Y. Perhaps it was anger. Here we are touching the
thorny problem of the message. It is quite possible that
my first drive was to protest. Yes. But if my work is
nothing but protest, then it's a failure. Picasso's "Guernica"
is a protest, but it is also a work of art. Otherwise, as
soon as the political context changed, it would have become
an advertisement, a placard, a poster. Now if "The

Prisoner" is nothing but a protest against the mistreatment of Palestinian villagers during the War of Independence, it should be consigned to oblivion. But I believe, I hope, that my work will be read and enjoyed by people who don't know what Arabs or Jews are, long after the conflict has become ancient history.

E. F. Most of your protagonists, including those in your recent Stories of the Plain, are youths, confronting the painful facts of life. Why?

S. Y. I really am not sure why this phase of life is so important to me. Perhaps because back when I was still very young, something grand, mysterious and complex happened in me. And still, to this day, I am trying to unravel the mystery, to untangle the knot. Perhaps when we're young, we feel more intensely and dare to respond to our innermost drives, whereas, as we grow older, we become less aware of our drives, or we are afraid to feel them. I suppose I feel that what happened then was so complex, awesome and profound that it deserves further treatment. I cannot permit myself to move on to the next phase. There is so much in a moment, a whole universe. I could write a whole book, even about this moment, right now, about the angle of the sun peering through the blinds, the way it illuminates this picture on the wall, the bubbling soda water in this glass. This is how I read, too. I keep returning to my favorite works. I read and reread them ten, fifteen, twenty times. I never get tired of rereading Proust, for example. Whenever I reread parts of A la recherche du temps perdu, I discover something new in the text.

A Jew reads and rereads the Psalter. The fiftieth time is very different from the tenth time. What do you know about a person after your first encounter with him? There is an endless scale of possibilities to know a person, and innumerable ways to listen to what he says, how he moves, why he does what he does.

Don Juan moved from one woman to another. To him, the first conquest was the most important one. Salvador Dali, on the other hand, saw in his wife a thousand women, because he knew how to perceive the differences and changes which transformed her from day to day, perhaps from hour to hour. In my writing I make love to every detail, I try to caress every aspect of every moment. That is why it's so difficult for me to write a novel. A novel moves from one period to another, from one phase to another. It is interested in development and transitions in time. A short story, on the other hand, depicts a situation in a given period of time. That's why The Days of Ziklag is a long short story (perhaps the longest every written) rather than a novel. You must develop a capability of sitting back and watching. If you are busy, if you have something on your mind, it won't work. To really be able to see, you must not look for anything. Leave your preconceived notions behind. The right state is an active passivity, where you relax, yet remain watchful and attentive. In your kind of work you probably have to read a lot, but what can you retain from a lot of books? What can become yours, truly and deeply? Montaigne said, there were only two authors he valued over all the rest, Plutarch and Seneca, because he never tired of drinking from their waters. They had the special salt which increased his thirst each time he took a sip.

E. F.   Do you find this kind of salt in your own writings?

S. Y.   Now this is a most cruel and painful question. No one knows the gap between that which I had wanted to achieve and what I managed to achieve, but I do. I hate the distance between the inspired picture of the imagination and its actualized version, pinned down to reality by those pale and fickle symbols we call words. Sometimes I have enormous compunctions, regret, guilt. I know where I have failed, where I could have done better. Perhaps this

24

is what writing is all about--the Sisyphean attempt to narrow the gap between the stirrings of the soul and the expressions of the mind.

E. F. You referred previously to Proust as your favorite writer. Which other authors or works have become "truly and deeply yours ?"

S. Y. First, let me explain that I see the concept of "influence" as an internal drama, rather than an external quality which is imposed on one's personality or self expression. We are "influenced" by something which is close and similar to the roots of our soul. Real influence is that which helps us be ourselves, that which elicits the hidden, the deepest secrets in us. John Ruskin exerted such influence on Proust. In my case it was Dickens. I first met his works as a teenager. I remember walking around, reciting pages and pages of Dickens from memory. Years later I realized how awful the Hebrew translation was. Nevertheless, Dickens managed to touch something very deep in me. The second was U. N. Gnessin. His style, his mode of writing, opened up to me the pathway toward myself and my own creativity.

E. F. Most authors ignore critics and literary theories.

S. Y. I became interested in literary criticism when I realized that people don't know how to read, and that the educational establishment increases the problem. Notes cannot make music, no matter how excellent they are. In order to produce music, the composer needs a musician, someone to bring the piece into reality. In literature also, much, very much depends on the reader. He is part of the artistic process. He realizes it with his perceptions, sensibilities, talent, understanding. Artistic reading, I think, is crucial for the progress and development of art.

25

It hurts me to hear readers dissect my <u>Days of Ziklag</u> in terms of material reality. It hurts me to see how they break up the holistic and harmonious work of art into its building blocks. Look at what the critics did to Agnon. They robbed his work of its mystery, of its appeal. They tried to explain him, returning him to the lowest level of communication, to history, to situations he had wanted to transform into something much higher, much more inspired. None of them hears Agnon's unique melody, the rhythm of his sentences.

E. F. You seem to be as interested in literary criticism as in creative writing, if not more. You published <u>Stories of the Plain</u> over a decade ago. Why did you abandon your creative writing?

S. Y. At present I am involved in literary theory. One day I will return to writing. But I knew it would come to this. Everyone wants to know why. As if we have answers for everything. In fact, the real great questions always remain unanswered. You do agree with me, don't you?

ITAMAR YAOZ-KEST

Itamar Yaoz-Kest was born in Hungary in 1934. During the Nazi occupation he was taken with his family to a concentration camp. His family returned to Hungary after the war when he resumed his studies at a Hebrew school. In 1951 he emigrated to Israel and entered a high school in Netania. He continued his education at the University of Tel Aviv. In 1960, he established the poetry monthly Eked, and since then he has been editor-in-chief of the Eked Publishing House. Itamar Yaoz-Kest has published several volumes of translated poetry, and won the Talpir prize for poetry in 1967.

His first book of poetry, Malakh lelo kenafaim (An Angel Without Wings) was published in 1959, followed by Nof be-ashan (Landscape in Smoke) 1961, Yerushat eynaim (A Heritage of Eyes) 1965, Shirim (Poems) 1967, Le-morad Beita (At The Foot of Her House) 1968, Du-shoresh (Dual Root) 1976. Among his fictional works are, Ba-halon ha-bait hanosea (At The Window of the Travelling House) 1970, Tsel ha-tsipor (The Shadow of a Bird) 1971, Ha-kav ha-zarhani (The Phosphorous Line) 1972, and Ahiza shel hol (A Grasp of Sand) 1977.

AUTHOR WITH A DUAL ROOT

An Interview with Itamar Yaoz-Kest*

E. F.   Your last two novels, The Shadow of the Bird and A
Grasp of Sand, and to a certain extent your first novel, In
the Window of the Traveling House, deal with the alienation
of a young Jewish writer, a holocaust survivor in Israel.
Why is this theme so central in your works?

I. Y. K.   I have dedicated my literary activity to the description of the painful experience of many immigrants, an experience which I was forced to suppress for a very long time,
and one which is denied or ignored by the mainstream of
contemporary writers, for obvious reasons.

E. F.   Can you describe this problem in greater detail?

I. Y. K.   Unlike immigrants to other countries, Jews who
come to Israel, immigrants back to their homeland, come
and expect to find a homeland--yet many of them feel foreign
here.   They struggle with a new environment, new values,
a new language.   At the same time they are pressured to
deny their childhood memories and to repress their past.
But without a past, one cannot live or create.

E. F.   How and why were you pressed to forget your past?

* Tel Aviv, August 1978.

28

I. Y. K. We are talking about extremely subtle things. This
is not a matter of institutional or political pressure, but
an implied, almost imperceptible one, which pervades
every aspect of Israel's cultural climate. I don't want to
be too categorical. Things may have changed somewhat
since the Yom Kippur war. Still, I remember that as a
teenager (I was sixteen when I arrived here) I was ashamed
to admit that I was from Hungary. I was jealous of the
strong, suntanned and gorgeous Sabra, and wanted to
imitate him in every possible way. I was the stooped,
pale Gola Jew, a victim. The condescending attitude of
the Israeli towards the immigrant Jew is a direct offshoot
of the revolt of Zionism against the Diaspora. The image
of the Jew as victim is offensive and threatening to the
Israeli ethos. Take, for instance, the apologetic title of
the day dedicated to the commemoration of the Holocaust,
"The Day of Holocaust and Heroism." What is the function
of heroism in this context? Probably to save the Jewish
honor. The Holocaust can serve as the most extreme
example, perhaps the ultimate symbol for the experience
of the Diaspora Jew and the way in which it is treated in
Israeli culture gives us a clue to the Israeli attitude toward
the whole issue of Diaspora Jewry.

E. F. How is it treated in Israeli culture?

I. Y. K. It is a mixture of embarrassment, fastidiousness
and solemnity. The catastrophe of World War 11 is not
approached as a historical and human phenomenon but as
a supernatural and demonic one--"the Nazi monster"--
"Satan"--"Hell"--the tendency is to mythologize the Holocaust and to present it as subhuman. The underlying premise
is that the Holocaust cannot be a legitimate subject in fiction
or art. Critics refuse to evaluate a novel about the Holocaust as a literary piece because for them the subject is
off limits. The work will become part of the dreary scene
of the commemoration days in high schools. Why wont

critics deal with these works objectively? Because no work can reproduce the horrors of the event. But who said that art is a reproduction of reality? If it were an exact reproduction, it would be history, journalism, not art. A painting is not and shouldn't be a photograph. The claim that the Holocaust is taboo in art comes from people who did not experience it personally. Holocaust survivors feel the exact opposite, that art revives something they want to bury in order to be able to cope with daily life. On the other hand, we must beware of the sensationalism we find in American productions on the Holocaust, which exploits the material in order to create titillations in the audience.

The Israeli evasion of the subject stems partly from a sense of guilt, but mainly from the desire to suppress the image of the Jew as victim. The trauma of the Yom Kippur war was produced not so much by the results of the war, as by their sudden proximity to the experience of the Holocaust. The shock was a result of confronting a reality in themselves, which most Israelis wish to deny.

The Holocaust for us was not over in 1945. It continues in the lives of the survivors and their children. We must stop denying this fact. Parents have effaced their own memories in order to make it easier for their children to adapt, and children have been ashamed to admit where their parents come from. But, as I said, the Holocaust is only a symbol, perhaps the most eloquent and most representative one, of the Jewish Diaspora experience.

E. F. In 1974 you published a pamphlet entitled The Neo-Jewish Outlook in Literature and Art. What is the meaning of the prefix "neo" in the title?

I. Y. K. What I was trying to express in the pamphlet was the perspective of those writers for whom Judaism was not a self evident fact, either in the religious or in the national-cultural scene. The majority of the writers who emigrated to Israel in the 1950s came from assimilated backgrounds.

I can give you an example from my own life. I grew up in
a Hungarian home whose Jewishness was little more than
lip-service to a Neological, or Reform, style of living.
In my Neological School, I learned how to read Hebrew from
a prayer book, but when one of my teachers wanted to intro-
duce Tefillin into the service, the parents' council demanded
that she be fired. Even after the Holocaust I was hardly
aware of my Jewish identity. My family returned to our
home town. I joined the Communist party and was dream-
ing of becoming a Hungarian poet. It was only after my
sister had settled in Israel that we decided to join her there.
My return to Israel is also a return to my Jewish identity,
to my language, heritage and culture. A full return to the
classical religious way of life is impossible for me (perhaps I do it vicariously through my religious wife). But
the adaptation to my own culture and language was a daily
struggle, and I can never take it for granted, the way
native Israeli writers do.

But the problems we were confronting were ignored.
Critics and literary scholars focused on the works of the
native authors, which they saw as mainstream Israeli
literature. This literature gave expression to the lassi-
tude of the second and third generation Israelis, who were
rebelling against the ideological and nationalistic writing
of their predecessors and sought individualistic avenues
of self expression. To them, social, national and collective
issues were boring and irrelevant. To us, these issues
were at the dead center of our personal lives and our
literary works.

I wanted to give a name to the struggles and frustrations
of a substantial group of writers who were all but ignored
because their concerns did not fit the individualistic,
decadent and aesthetic vogue in Israeli literature. David
Avidan and Nathan Zach in poetry and A. B. Yehoshua,
Amos Oz and Amalia Kahana-Carmon in prose fiction
gave expression to the bankruptcy of social ideals and

31

national values, while we were struggling to understand and articulate these values in our first encounter with them. While the mainstream artists tried to be inventive, original and shocking at all costs, and while they looked for the most effective or iconoclastic literary forms, we were trying to articulate our pain. What mattered to us was substance.

E. F. In A Grasp of Sand, the protagonist, a young immigrant writer, admits that he feels hostile toward two kinds of people--those whose mother tongue is Hebrew, and those who continued to use their native language without adapting to the new language. To what extent does this confession reflect your own experience as a young writer in Israel?

I. Y. K. All my novels are based on personal experience, though they are not strictly autobiographical. My struggle with the language is perhaps the best metaphor for the more encompassing encounter with my new identity. For many years I did everything to efface my past. I was afraid to touch books in Hungarian. I repressed nursery rhymes, silly puns, tunes, all the things which make up one's associative landscape. But my biological root could not be completely eradicated. It persisted in my subconscious. I closed the door on my past, but it crept back in through the window.

Every person is born into a given language in which he perceives the first scenes of his life, and in which he gives form to his first perceptions. He continues to grow, think, dream and write in this language. Consciously, I worked in Hebrew, but subliminally my language was different.

But it's not only language. One day I walked down the street and heard someone call, "Peter, Peter," which is my original name. I didn't respond. I later found out that it was my cousin from England, who hadn't seen me for twenty years and hadn't been aware of my new name.

But it's not only the name. In "A Nightly Seduction" I
described the fear of being captured by childhood books.
The end of the poem:

> . . .volumes in my banished mother tongue
> to return my love to them,
> seize me,
> and carry my body to the door,
> while you're asleep
> the children in bed,
> and outside
> chilly winds rise--
> and I am afraid to betray myself
> with a scream,
> for I don't know the language in which I dream at night.
>   (Translation: E. F.)

Sometimes I am overwhelmed by an irrational dread---
what if the language I abandoned takes revenge on me?

E. F.   Is this the underlying motif of A Dual Root?

I. Y. K.   This is the underlying theme of most of my works,
and those of many writers who emigrated after World War 11,
such as Shimon Balas, Ya'akov Besser, Shamai Golan,
Dan Pagis, Erez Biton, Uri Orlev, Reuven Ben-Yosef,
and to a large extent Aharon Appelfeld. Despite the
enormous differences in culture and background (Balas
is from Iraq, Ben-Yosef from the United States, Besser
from Poland), they all share a dual root. They were all
taught to be ashamed of their birthplace and repress their
ties with their original root. Although they give expression
to the experiences of the majority of the people in the
country, their writings are considered peripheral.
     The critical attitude which focuses on the native writers
at the expense of the dual-rooted ones is destructive because it turns the Israeli literary scene into a monolithic
and unexciting area. The fact is that this country bursts
with problems and events which beg to be written about, and

yet you keep finding the same themes in the mainstream works, as if nothing else existed. You will not find in them reference to the conflict between secular and religious lifestyles. The only exception I can think of is Miriam Schwartz's The Story of Hava Gottlieb, which in fact continues the familiar plot line of escape from religion to a secular world. What about the opposite trend, which is of course peripheral, yet extremely interesting? The move away from the Jewish sources complements the transition away from the historical experience of the Jews in the Diaspora. It started as early as the 1920s.

E. F. What about Agnon?

I. Y. K. Agnon was an exception. In fact, Agnon was considered a peripheral phenomenon in the 1920s and 1930s. He came into prominence only in old age. I remember the times when Avigdor Hameiri was much more prominent than Agnon.

E. F. How does this move away from the traditional past affect the quality of literature in Israel?

I. Y. K. It does not affect poetry as much as it affects the novel, because poetry does not need a historical perspective. Perhaps I should clarify that I see a difference between poetry which is the sum total of a poet's work, a framework in which you can perceive a world, a totality, and a poem which is a unit or aspect of this world. Anyway, a poem is a product of an immediate and direct encounter with the environment. It is based on a personal, emotional and spontaneous response to the present. In many ways, the swift changes in mood, and the hectic swinging of the historical pendulum in Israel, stimulate poetic activity. Indeed, Israeli contemporary poets, I dare say, reached a level unparalleled by some of our most talented prose writers. On the other hand, if one tries to employ the

materials of our contemporary reality in a novel, it may
smack of journalism. An immediate response to events is
destructive in a novel, which is primarily a work evolving
in time, and which juxtaposes several perceptions of the
same thing from different points of view. Prose writing
requires a historical or, if you want, aesthetic distance.
By renouncing the Jewish past, Israeli authors lose a
temporal dimension which is crucial for the novel. I think
it's not a coincidence that some of the better works in
Hebrew literature are historical, such as the works of
Kabak and some of Shamir.

E. F. Amos Oz's novella, Unto Death, treats the Middle
Ages.

I. Y. K. But it's inauthentic. You can sense that he was
more concerned with the style of his sentences than with
the subject matter. This is a good example of bad literature,
an exploitation of a historical problem for cheap sensationalism and aesthetic effect, and I don't think he made
even aesthetic conquests in his work. Bad lines of poetry
do not make good lines in prose.

E. F. What is your definition of good literature?

I. Y. K. In my opinion, there are three basic criteria for
judging literature--originality, integrity and authenticity.
The first one is most troublesome, because it depends
exclusively on historical circumstances, literary generations, trends, vogues, etc. H. N. Bialik was definitely
innovative. He broke away from the style of Y. L. Gordon.
This, however, isn't what makes him great. The second
criterion is more important. Here, the question is whether
the artistic work includes all the necessary elements and
whether certain elements are expendable. The most important criterion, in my opinion, is authenticity. Here,
the reader must judge whether the work materializes the

reality it pretends to materialize. Now, of course, a person who is insensitive to certain scenes, emotions, moods or problems in reality, would not be able to respond to them when they are invoked in a literary work. It's like describing colors to a blind man. The contemporary writers and critics are too concerned with the first criterion, innovativeness. Authors and poets try to be outrageous and scandalous at all costs, to shock the numb reader out of his slumber. A voguish element to serve this purpose is sex, sex for the sake of sensationalism. You find convoluted structures and sophisticated forms, all this wriggling and squirming before you can read a truthful sentence. Most of the creative energy is wasted on superficialities.

E. F. What about authenticity?

I. Y. K. The way I see it is this. Truly great literature grows out of a crisis. The Russians created a great literature because they were open to and aware of their distress, and mind you, distress doesn't have to be economic or social. Sylvia Plath's Bell Jar is an authentic expression of distress, in an affluent society. Now compare this to My Michael! What is needed is a sensitivity to pain. In Israel, there are two possible directions for good fiction. The one revolves around the conflict between fathers and sons, especially among the native Israelis. The second direction is the conflict of the immigrant with his new environment. But very little has been written about either of these problems.

E. F. What about Yehoshua's Early in The Summer of 1970, or even Amos Oz's Lands of The Jackal?

I. Y. K. Yes, you can find here genuine attempts to depict decadence, perhaps even a certain measure of insight into the process of degeneration. Still, the impact, the depth of the pain is missing. Look, I am not just criticizing

36

for the sake of criticizing. I do it with a very acute consciousness of my own limitations. The fact is that contemporary Israeli literature is monopolized by a coterie
of native writers, whose scope and achievements are
rather limited. It is hard to find among them one who
managed to realize a world. Appelfeld did it. But what
is the world of Yehoshua, or Oz? I am critical of them
because they are talented and could achieve much more
had they been more open to their own distress, the pain of
their own society. I'll give you an example. A few years
ago I published a posthumous volume of poems by Ido Ben-
Gurion, a young man, who became a drug addict and sub-
sequently committed suicide. Ido was the grandson of
Berdichevsky. I see something symbolic and inevitable
in this fact. Now, Ido was no genius, but his poems shook
me up. I saw in them an abyss, something I didn't experience in the works of the mainstream writers. They write
about the breakdown and bankruptcy of values, but they
seem to skirt the issue. They fail to shake me up.

E. F.   Can't comic literature be great as well?

I. Y. K.   Laughter spreads ripples on the surface, tears
come from inside. A painter once told me, many years
ago, that a work which does not bring tears to one's eyes
is not art. At that time, I thought this was schmaltz, but
later I realized that he was right. Art must hurt. First,
it must hurt the artist himself, the artist must experience
pain before he creates. Otherwise, he won't be able to
produce tears. A true artist must describe the things he
is most afraid of, all that which he wants to avoid.

E. F.   In my opinion, Israeli literature is frightfully serious,
and to a great extent it lost the comic perspective of the
great Yiddish writers.

I. Y. K.   We must distinguish between the laughter of

37

entertainment, or recreational laughter, and laughter which
is the flip side of tears. Pain is not necessarily evoked by
a tearful scene, or physical wounds. Tolstoy can hurt you
with a scene at a party. A tragedy is not necessarily an
expression of pessimism. The creative act is a confirma-
tion of life and a belief in continuity. Proust can describe
an abhorrent scene, but it would be beautiful as a piece
of literature. In real life, a broken jar is useless. In art,
it is the broken jar and not the perfect one which is interesting. Segal wrote his Love Story out of a certain cynicism.
He knew better than that. What a genuine author must
avoid at all costs is a "nice" or "cute" work. This is the
worst affront to art.

E.F. What is the way out of the deadlock?

I.Y.K. A greater openness to a variety of subjects, problems and experiences. A greater attentiveness to authors
of different backgrounds, even to writers in Israel who use
their native languages. A very important literature in
Yiddish, Polish, French, and Spanish--even English--is
growing here, unnoticed. Authors like Oded Sverdlick,
R. Rubin, G. Urbach, Claude Vige, Richard Flantz,
Elisheva Senesh, and many others write about their experiences in Israel, some of them from a non-Jewish perspective. Why is Gabriel Preil, who sits in New York and
writes in Hebrew, considered one of the important poets
in Israeli literature, whereas those who made a conscious
decision to settle in Israel are ignored by the literary establishment? If Israeli literature wishes to grow and become a landmark in world literature, it ought to become
more pluralistic--more heterogeneous and more aware of
its own potentials.

ABRAHAM B. YEHOSHUA

A. B. Yehoshua, as he is commonly known, was born in
Jerusalem in 1936, but has made his home in Haifa for some
time now where there is an energetic Arab Israeli literary
community, in which he has shown interest. He graduated
from Rehaviah High School, after which he studied Hebrew
literature and philosophy at Hebrew University. He re-
eived his B.A. degree in 1961, and graduated from
Teacher's College in 1962. Yehoshua taught in high school
from 1961-1963, when he left for Paris to serve as high
school director for a year, and as the general secretary of
the World Association of Jewish Students until 1967. He
was lecturer at the University of Haifa from 1967-1972,
dean of students from 1972-1977; and from 1977 professor
of literature. He has also been a visiting lecturer in several
universities in England and the United States.

An active member of the Labor Party, he has published
regularly political essays, and has given frequent lectures
on Zionism and Judaism, some of which are included in
his book of essays on the Arab-Israeli conflict, Bi-zekhut
ha-hormaliut, 1980 (Between Right and Right: tr. Arnold
Schwartz, 1981). Yehoshua has also served as a member
of the editorial board of the literary journal Keshet, and at
present is a contributing editor of Siman Keri'a.

Yehoshua started to publish stories in 1957. His first
collection, Mot ha-zaken (Death of An Old Man) appeared
in 1963. Among the books that followed are Mul ha-
ye'arot (Facing the Forests) 1968; Three Days and A
Child, 1970; Bithilat kayits 1970, in 1972 (Early In The
Summer of 1970, published in English in 1977); Hame'ahev,
1977 (The Lover, 1979); Gerushim Me'u harim (A Late
Divorce) 1982. "Facing The Forests" appears in Modern
Hebrew Literature, edited by Robert Alter, 1975.

IDEOLOGY AND LITERATURE

An Interview with A.B. Yehoshua*

E.F. Avraham Ben Yehoshua, do you consider your first
very popular novel, The Lover, as a breakthrough in your
writing career?

A.B.Y. First, let me tell you, this popularity is a little
embarrassing. Here, in Israel, as you know, writing is
an ideal, a vocation, a social responsibility, a goal in life.
When it becomes a lucrative business too, it's confusing,
one doesn't quite know how to take it. My previous work
enjoyed mostly a critical success, not in absolute terms
of course, some pieces were controversial, but on the
whole, I can say, I was pampered by the critics--I didn't
exactly suffer from lack of attention. The Lover, however,
reached an audience which I never hoped to reach--colleagues
who never read Hebrew literature, professors of law and
international relations, a psychiatrist, neighbors, my
wife's cosmetician. Everyone seems to find in the book
what he or she is able to or wants to find there. It dramatizes for me the fallacy of objective reading.

   With all the differences in the critical reviews I got,
they all seemed to have more or less the same style--
disciplined, academic, with a pretension to objectivity.
Here, I am getting reactions from non-professionals,
and to me this is very revealing. But, to return to your
question, I definitely see The Lover as a breakthrough.

* Jerusalem, August, 1978.

As you said, this is my first novel. It took me a long time, about twenty years, to feel ready for it. It is a more serious and far more difficult undertaking than a short story. It involves a greater sensitivity to details and to different points of view. It requires a perspective, a Weltanschauung. That doesn't mean, of course, that a novel will, by definition, be good or better than one's short stories. Nevertheless, there is something in the sheer size difference, in the greater quantitative comprehensiveness of a novel, which places it on a different qualitative level. Whom do you remember from the nineteenth century? Tolstoy, Dostoevski, Balzak, Zola, Dickens--novelists--people who brought to life and created a reality. Of course, to be fair, add your token poet. All right, we'll add Beaudelaire to the list.

E. F. Is literary criticism important, in your opinion?

A. B. Y. I think that the serious criticism, the one which is interested in deeper developments and global trends and tendencies, is very important. This kind of criticism is very different from journalistic review, which evaluates a certain work superficially and tends to serve personal grudges more often than lofty ideas. Unfortunately, many of our serious critics stopped treating the contemporary scene. With the exception of Gershon Shaked, most of them (Dan Meiron, Eli Schweid, Benjamin Hrushovski) are involved in other areas.

E. F. Why did you write The Lover?

A. B. Y. I simply wanted to describe an experience of a group of people in a certain situation, specific individuals, their dreams and desires and distinct personalities facing a certain reality. If you find ideology here, on the upper levels, all right. But the foundation remains--characters in relation to a certain situation. I create a certain link between them and myself, and I try to describe what's happening to them.

E.F. Who are these characters? How were they created?

A.B.Y. They may be combinations of several people I know in reality. Some are purely imaginary, no models involved. This reminds me of a girl, a friend, who after a visit to Africa told me that what I described in "A Long Summer Day: His Despair, His Wife and His Daughter," the atmosphere and social context of the Israeli experts in Africa were precisely what she saw there. I have, of course, never visited Africa. But in The Lover, I treat people and places which everyone meets everywhere, or may meet, or will--a school teacher, a mechanic, a garage, an Arab teenager.

E.F. In "Facing the Forests" you describe a peculiar relationship between a Jewish Israeli ranger and an Arab mute. Many interpreted the story as a political allegory about Israel and the Arabs. What is the function of Naim in The Lover?

A.B.Y. Naim is one of the characters in the novel. He is not different from Adam or Dafi, or anyone else. He happens to be an Arab. Just because he is Arab, one needn't label him as such to the exclusion of his other traits. He is first and foremost a teenager, with thoughts, wishes, emotions and problems. As to the Arab in "Facing the Forests" he is a minor figure, quite peripheral. I didn't attempt to flesh him out. His presence in the story is very different from Naim's presence in the novel.

E.F. Why did you choose the monologic form in which the characters, rather than the narrator, report on the plot progression?

A.B.Y. First, this format afforded me an easy transition from the short story to the novel. I also wanted to show that everyone of us sees reality in a radically different way, that it is in fact impossible to talk about a certain reality, since it depends on one's point of view. A Jewish mechanic and an Arab youth see the same events or the same object, in a radically different way. Juxtaposing the incongruous perspectives in the same context dramatizes this point. The format may also suggest something about the breakdown of the narrator's authority.

E.F. You seem to draw a sharp and clear demarcation between your political ideology and your literary activity. Why?

A.B.Y. I think that ideology is very dangerous in art, though lately I realize that the separation between the two is almost inevitable. In my first works, I was very careful to make the distinction. Now, it is difficult to be political in the market place and artistic at home. Of course, the ideal would be to use ideology as an artistic vehicle. The great authors succeded in doing it. In Dostoevski, for example, the ideology of the protagonist is an expression of his psychological makeup. Here, ideology and psychology complement and emphasize each other. Since ideology is part of the human personality, it deserves a place in the kingdom of eternal truths. But as authors we must be careful to record only the essence, the unchanging truth of the actuality we are introducing into our work. Otherwise, we turn literature into a prostitute, a servant of journalism and politics.

E.F. As a political thinker, how do you envision the future of the Arab-Israeli conflict?

A.B.Y. The future--who knows? The future may be rather bleak. Israel may become like Northern Ireland, where two nations live side by side, and continue to sharpen the edges of their conflict, and deepen the cultural and political gap between them. There is only a slight chance that the Arabs will leave us alone, and let us live in peace, so we won't have to be obsessed by the conflict between us, and be able to live with our own problems. Maybe the Jewish identity which was fostered in the Diaspora will start dissolving a bit, and a new identity will crystallize out of the peaceful coexistence with the Arabs, a Hebraic-Israeli identity, unique, yet tolerant, not nationalistic and not fanatic. This process had begun, but because of the repeated wars it suffered setbacks, and continues to regress. In a state of national conflict, people tend to cling to superficial labels and fanatic expressions of identity. This is what happens with the new religious fanaticism and neo-Judaic trend of Itamar Yaoz-Kest. The neo-Judaism of the European immigrants is a reaction against a basically non-existent reality. Yaoz-Kest and Appelfeld were supposedly traumatized by their encounter with the New Israeli, the omnipotent undefeated Sabra. However, this stereotype is to a large extent their own projection. It's enough to read Yizhar's Days of Ziklag to see that this image is totally fabricated. At any rate, now, after the Yom Kippur War, the myth of the Sabra superman has been undermined, and the Jewish tears and lamentations have returned to their former respectable place.

E. F. It seems to me that the plaintive tone, bemoaning the gap between the Zionist ideal and its realization is one of the most characteristic features of Israeli fiction.

A. B. Y. Every literature tends to be a bit lachrymose. It always deplores the loss of Eden, it always mourns the Fall. Every national literature has a distant golden and perfect past, whether historical or fictional, the loss of which it mourns. It's a general phenomenon; Israeli literature is part of it.

44

E. F.   It is possible to trace a steady progression in your writing towards what I would call, for lack of a better term, greater concreteness.   Each successive work, from the first allegories of "Death of An Old Man,"through "Early in The Summer of 1970,"to The Lover features more of the specific Israeli context in which the stories take place. Are you aware of this development?

A. B. Y.   If there is a greater measure of concreteness in my later work, it is because I want to deepen my characters, to flesh them out, to give them more body, and more space in which to grow.   The local color is meant to focus and sharpen their experiences and moods, not vice versa. My aim is not to reproduce the Israeli or any other reality. There are authors whose aim is mainly to describe a historical reality, including its special types, customs, manners and mores.   This is not my aim.   I use a specific context about which I write in order to reflect something fixed and eternal in the human condition.   The most important thing for me is to discover the underlying general idea beneath the incidental and variegated details.   But my movement towards greater fullness and totality of specific backgrounds stems, I think, from the need, the desire, not to impose the abstract idea or insight on the reality, but to let the reality grow naturally, and dramatize the idea at the same time.   My first protagonists reflected a very important part of myself, a sense of solitude, foreignness, and a radical alienation from the here and now. I am not so interested in the concrete description of the environment, but I am ready to come to terms with other aspects in me, with those aspects which are involved with my environment.

E. F.   Were your first allegories an attempt to protest against the social realism of the early fifties?

A. B. Y.   The Palmach generation was comprised of

different authors. It depends on the specific authors. I admired--and still do admire--the work of S. Yizhar. The rest I admire less. Again, it depends on the specific works. Many of the Palmach authors grew, developed and changed. Aharon Megged and Moshe Shamir, for example. Nevertheless, I admit that there still exists a basic difference between Hanoch Bartov, Nathan Shacham and Shamir, on the one hand, and myself, Amos Oz, Amalia Kahana-Carmon and Aharon Appelfeld, on the other. Something in their world view didn't quite work for us. There was too much solidarity with the public line, too much conformity and adherence to the prevailing national ideology. They endorsed the dominant collective values too readily, they lived with a full commitment to collectively sanctioned ideas, whereas we searched for the side streets, the alleys. We were more interested in the periphery.

Despite the changes in the writings of the Palmach authors, one can still identify a certain moral code as its basic frame of reference. Their heroes are still shocked and disappointed by the breakdown of moral and collective values. This doesn't mean that we are less interested in our society, nation and culture. It depends, of course, on the definition of these things. I think that my generation is closer in many ways to those who preceded the Palmach authors. Amos Oz, for example, is very close to Berdichevsky. Amalia Kahana-Carmon's writing reminds me of Gnessin, not so much in her style as in her insight.

E. F. Who was your own main inspiration?

A. B. Y. Unquestionably Agnon, especially his surrealistic stories. Today, I am not as enchanted with The Book of Deeds as I used to be, but in the beginning, he was the one who inspired me to write my first stories. I think his influence is obvious in Death of An Old Man.

E. F. An additional development in your writing is a

greater openness to spoken Hebrew. Your first stories employed--shall we say--a more formal written style.

A.B.Y.   It seems to me that the style should change according to the subject matter, form, etc. Style must serve the specific work. Agnon's unchanged style of writing, for example, stifled him in many ways. His stylistic purity, which I tend to see as sterility, dried him up. The dialogues in Shira are artificial and unconvincing. In the mouth of a German secular professor, or an Oriental maid, Mishnaic Hebrew just doesn't come off. Many authors refuse to change their style, and continue to play on a single chord. Fine. I'm not criticizing. But it's permissible to move to another wave length. I don't regret my move to what you call "spoken Hebrew," though I am not quite sure that this is the right definition. In many instances I create an illusion of spoken Hebrew, though in reality, the words I employ are not likely to appear in a natural dialogue. The test is not whether people actually speak this way, but whether it sounds authentic. A fish in a painting does not have to fit in size, shape and color to a fish in reality. Authenticity is not tested in technical terms. Take for example Amalia's "Ne'ima Sasson Writes Poems." The fourteen year old girl uses words one must look up in a dictionary, yet it is authentic. The verisimilitude remains intact. Stylistic flexibility is essential for one's development and continued vigor.

E.F.   Do you find anything in common with Jewish writers outside of Israel?

A.B.Y.   Not really. I like Bellow, I think he has something to say. But I don't read him because he is Jewish, but because he is good. I prefer Faulkner to most of the other Jewish authors in America, and though I know very little about the Blacks, his work appeals to me much more than, say, Malamud's work.

E. F. To what extent does the Jewish or Israeli element
play a role in your writing?

A. B. Y. To the extent that I am Jewish and Israeli. But
I fail to see the distinction between "Jewish" and "Israeli."
You know, you remind me of that critic Baumgarten, an
American Jew, or a Jewish American, whatever they call
themselves. Do you know what he said? He said he liked
my novel qua novel. What he did not like was the fact that
it was not Jewish enough. Now can you imagine such hum-
bug? If Bernard Malamud writes about a Jewish shopkeeper
in New York, he is automatically categorized as a "Jewish
writer"; but if I write about a Jewish mechanic in Tel Aviv,
my novel is "not Jewish enough." I am sorry, I can't follow
the logic. To me, The Lover is a Jewish book, just as much
as, if not more than, The Assistant or The Fixer. Why?
Because it was written in the State of Israel, and because
it was written in Hebrew.

E. F. Is the writing of Saul Bellow, Philip Roth or Bernard
Malamud less Jewish because it's in English and in the
United States?

A. B. Y. Frankly, I don't think the Jewish element in
Bellow is all that important. What is so Jewish about
Roth? These are American writers who by the very fact
of their living in America have made a conscious choice
not to partake in the most dramatic Jewish struggle for
survival in modern times, the struggle which is going on
in Israel. They write out of an American reality, within
an American culture, to American readers. Their lives
aren't threatened, their right to the land is not questioned,
their safety is not challenged. Theirs is an affluent
society, they can take for granted so many things we must
fight long and hard to get. So, really, I don't consider
them Jewish writers, but writers who happened to be born
to Jewish parents, and I don't think they will be pleased if

you tell them otherwise.

E. F.   At the same time, the Jewish element is not too strong in your own works.

A. B. Y.   First, we must be clear about this term, which has been too long and too much misunderstood. What do you mean by "Jewish"! If you equate it with "religious," then I'm willing to concede--my stories are nothing of the kind. But to me, Judaism is far deeper and more encompassing than a synonym for a certain religious set of values and creeds. This definition was fostered by generations of Diaspora Jews for obvious reasons--it exempted them from the responsibility to pack up and go to Israel. Now, their descendants, the Jews of Long Island, think of themselves as faithful Jews because they care to drive up to temple once a week, or park the car around the block if it happens to be a Conservative synagogue. But from us, Israelis, they demand a poster, a symbol. They are very angry when we fail to fulfill their expectations, to realize their utterly fabricated definition of Judaism. And we naively and stupidly swallow their definition, and end up with an upset stomach. We have been contaminated with the galut sickness.

E. F.   What is this sickness?

A. B. Y.   It's a collective mental sickness. Did you ever see a person who always dreams of living somewhere but never cares to actually see or visit that place? Diaspora Jews remind me of the man who built himself a house on the beach. After nightly nightmares he scrupulously checks the house to see how much water has penetrated. How much assimilation has managed to corrode the edges! The tragic paradox is that we here in Israel have contracted this germ. Why, look at the endless arguments about "Jewish" versus "Israeli" identity, as if there is any difference between the

49

two. I have nothing against those who renounce their Jewish identity, and assimilate. But those who consider themselves committed Jews are involved in a perverse masochistic game. They live in the Diaspora and pledge allegiance, lip service, to Israel, repeating, "Next year in Jerusalem," knowing full well that they don't mean it. They accept the Jewish classical ideology against the Diaspora, yet ignore it. Why don't they create new ideologies and new texts?

E.F. What is the most important asset of a writer?

A.B.Y. For me, the most important thing is to be able to delve into my innermost abysses, and expose whatever I find there, without fear. The most important thing is the ability to expose one's innermost secrets. I don't mean in a factual, biographical sense, of course. The ability to conquer one's terror, and record everything, including the most revolting truths in one's being.

E.F. We began our conversation with the enthusiastic reception of The Lover. What do you think of the Israeli readership, in general?

A.B.Y. Keeping in mind the political condition and the size of the country and the population, Israel has one of the most dynamic reading publics in the world. We must remember that the mother tongue of a large percentage here is not Hebrew. I know that critics complain and worry. But, all things considered, the Israelis are avid readers, they care and react with great zeal, and there is no need to criticize.

E.F. The allegorical element of your work invites much speculation. Several works have received conflicting interpretations. Is it important to you that the reader should understand your stories?

A.B.Y. Understanding is an intellectual activity. I don't think that my work is a riddle which ought to be decoded. I think of it more in terms of sensations. If the reader experiences the story, if I manage to elicit certain feelings in him, my goal is accomplished.

E. F. Is the response of readers to your work important to you?

A.B.Y. Though some authors may tell you they don't care about the public appeal of their books, I think that we all want to impress our readers and to be accepted by them. If an artist has something to say, he wants to be heard and he wants to create a lasting impression. If he believes in the value of his insight, he wants it published, publicized and remembered. I am not different.

AHARON APPELFELD

In many ways, Aharon Appelfeld's life is symbolic of
the Jewish journey from Europe to Israel. Born into an
assimilated family in Bukovnia in 1932, he and his family
were exported to the labor camp of Transnistria during the
Nazi occupation. He himself escaped from the camp when
he was eight years old, and for the next three years
wandered through the forests of Poland with other bands
of children. He was picked up by the Red Army in 1944,
and pressed into kitchen service in the Ukraine, after which
he made his way to Italy, and finally to Palestine in 1946.
He studied Hebrew and Yiddish literature at Hebrew University, served in the Israeli army, and presently teaches
literature at the Haim Greenberg College in Jerusalem.

Appelfeld's first collection of stories Ashan (Smoke) was
published in 1963. In 1965 he published Kefor al ha-arets
(Frost on the Land). His other publications include:
Be-komat hakarka (On The First Floor) 1968; Ha-or veha-
kutonet (The Skin and the Garment) 1971; Ke-ishon ha-ain
(Like The Pupil of The Eye); Badenheim 1939 published in
1981; and his most recent book to appear in English: Tor
hapelaot, 1978 (The Age of Wonders, 1981).

But To Me These Roots Are Lost Forever

Interview with Aharon Appelfeld
(Jerusalem, August, 1978)

He is considered one of Israel's most important authors, but is still surprised when asked for an interview. For an American journal? But so few of his works have been translated into English! He is lazy and inefficient when it comes to publicity matters. His novella, <u>Like</u> <u>The</u> <u>Pupil</u> <u>of</u> <u>the</u> <u>Eye</u>, was recently translated, but "even the average Israeli reader has a hard time with my stories."

E. F. Why do you think so?

A. A. My stories are not sensational. Many of them lack a plot. I tend to minimize and reduce rather than exaggerate things. I cannot offer anything titillating, shocking, or extravagant. Art usually attempts to accentuate and dramatize the facts of life as much as possible. I go in the opposite direction.

E. F. You are known as the "Poet of the Holocaust," yet your works never speak directly of what happened during the war. Most characters of <u>In</u> <u>the</u> <u>Blooming</u> <u>Vale</u> and <u>Frost</u> <u>on</u> <u>Earth</u> are vagrant survivors in Europe. The protagonist of <u>The</u> <u>Skin</u> <u>and</u> <u>the</u> <u>Garment</u> is a Holocaust survivor in Israel.

A. A. I am not a historian of the Holocaust. I am not interested in describing the events that took place. I could not have done so even if I had wanted to. How can one describe the thing itself? Can art ever compete with life?

All I am trying to do is to elicit certain universal and eternal elements from the historical event. I want to learn from it something about us, human beings of all times and in different situations.

E. F. You were thirteen when you first emigrated to Israel, yet all of your works, from <u>Smoke,</u> your first collection of short stories, to your last novella, <u>Years</u> <u>and</u> <u>Hours,</u> seem to revolve around the Holocaust. Why?

A.A. I was seven years old when the war broke out. My elementary school was the concentration camp of Transniestra. What I saw and learned there was the only formal education I received. I never even went to school once I arrived here. I saw something which I am still trying to comprehend, or at least to deal with, through art. I am in Israel now, and it is a new reality. But my innermost self is still there. In this respect, I don't think I am different from most Israelis, who are basically immigrants. Their children might have been born here, but the immigrant consciousness is transferred to them as well. The unified educational system and the army seem to be powerful formative factors, but not as powerful as memories and cultural roots.

E. F. Your mother tongue is German. Did you find it difficult to write in Hebrew?

A.A. Learning the language is to me an unending process. I took my first formal lesson in Hebrew literature at Hebrew University. I guess this accounts for my relatively late start. On the other hand, I can still savor the sounds of the language in a way that a native Israeli may not be able to. I attach great importance to the sound of the word, to the cadence of a sentence, to the melody of a paragraph. A story is not only meaning, it's music as well. I want my stories to be read out loud.

E. F.   By continually evoking the Holocaust in your stories, are you trying to tell people they must not forget?

A. A.   I am not an ideologist or a preacher. (He pauses. He puffs on his pipe thoughtfully.) You know, one of the great critics said, "God resides in the details." (He emits a short, quiet laugh.) I am only a recorder of details.

E. F.   The characters in your stories, did you meet them or invent them?

A. A.   Every one of my works is based on a personal experience. Can art be completely invented? It's a matter of shaping reality with the help of imagination. I am not interested in presenting an external reality. The characters I shape are my internal reality, they exist in my mind, you won't find them in the "real world." After all, I am working with fiction.

E. F.   The people you depict seem constantly to be wandering from one place to the other, even when not persecuted. A pervasive restlessness dominates their lives.

A. A.   Those who survived the war will never be able to return to what we call a normal life. It sometimes does not show on the surface. Many survivors seem to have found their niche, a new purpose. The truth is that they repress the memories, the guilt, the terror. Normal life for a survivor is an absurdity. My characters are restless because they are haunted by guilt: why did I deserve to survive and others had to die? Am I better than they? Smarter? There is an inexplicable, an irrational feeling that we betrayed those who stayed behind. What is the nature of the force which condemned them to death while granting me life?

But there is another answer to your question. Paradoxically, the survivors are seeking something they had in the

war and which now seems to be lost forever--the feeling of
solidarity and mutual responsibility. When the external
pressure let up, friendships dissolved, groups broke up,
and brotherhood was exposed as a mere illusion. So that
the end of the war brought about yet another, albeit paradoxical, disappointment. The individual was hurled into a
reality dominated by competition and egotistical indifference.
He is not in physical danger, but he is still haunted by his
memories and his solitude.

E. F. In these descriptions, are you drawing on a personal
experience you underwent after the war?

A. A. The personal element is not interesting. What
matters is the way in which it is molded in art, isn't it?

E. F. What is the universal situation you wanted to dramatize in your description of aimless wanderings?

A. A. A person who undergoes a traumatic experience
believes that he shares a common destiny with those who
experience the same trauma. He expects the same solidarity and intimacy which characterized his life with the
others under the shadow of death, to continue. Naturally,
these expectations are not realized, for this is the nature
of expectations in general. His illusion is dispelled. I
think this does not describe only what happened in the past,
specifically to Holocaust survivors. This experience is at
the root of human existence, and I believe it is relevant now
and will always be. There are moments of intimacy,
friendship and solidarity, which intensify under external
pressure, then they disappear. The hope for a continued
brotherhood is lost. One loses his sense of direction and
doesn't know where or why.

E. F. Some of your characters, like Chuhovsky in "The
Islands of St. George" retreat into solitude, leaving society

and turning to nature.

A.A. What should a person do after the Holocaust--sit in
an armchair and read a paper? After Auschwitz, should
he go to the market and buy tomatoes, or teach at the
university? Normal life is absurd, normal relationships
are pedestrian, stupid, senseless, idiotic. Those people
who seem to return to normal life pay a price. They take
the past and hide it deep in their souls. On the other hand,
to continue to live in the past is just as impossible. One's
life becomes a fluctuation between absurdities.

E.F. Did you ever try, perhaps in your unpublished work,
to draw on the Israeli dilemma? Did you ever try to use
Israel as a meaningful framework for your writing?

A.A. What is Israel? This country's population consists
of 60-70 percent immigrants whose immediate present un-
folds here, but their inner life, their roots are in another
place, the place they came from. There is, of course, a
thin layer of natives, who were born here, but they too have
their roots planted in their parents. I am searching for my
roots. I think this is the primary role of an author--if one
is interested in the surface he can avail himself of a camera.

E.F. It seems that lately there is a greater receptivity to
literature about the Holocaust. Does this have any meaning for you?

A.A. Art is a lonely occupation. I can't say that my writing didn't get response in the past. After all, I was writing
about something which many people were aware of. I didn't
have to start from the beginning. But I wanted to confront
it through form. I didn't want to teach new things, but to
mold what was known, to give it shape. An artist is tested
by his details: how he builds a sentence, the comma between
words, the choice of the words, this is the test of authenticity,

the authenticity of the details. There is no other criterion. My message is in the sentence, its tone, its structure.

E. F. Your style tends to be, what one might call for lack of a better term, "poetic." Your descriptions of scenery are extensive, the imagery is rich, and the use of metaphors frequent. Did you try to write poetry?

A. A. In the beginning, yes. But I didn't persist in it. In so far as my descriptions are concerned, I guess I try to describe the fullness of the moment, to capture the moment with all its hues, moods and suggestiveness.

E. F. One figure which recurs in some of your stories is the Jewish child, abandoned or thrown into a monastery, such as Berta or Kitty. What does this experience mean to you?

A. A. Many Holocaust survivors felt responsible for the others--it's a matter of moral commitment. Many feel guilty for abandoning the others. The motif of abandoning a child in a monastery symbolizes for me one of the most terrifying possibilities--cutting off one's roots. I come from an assimilated family. The Holocaust has taught me what it means to be part of a tribe, a member of a community. One of the most vicious ironies of World War 11 is the fact that most Jews didn't even know why they were being punished. Most of them saw themselves as an integral part of their society, as equal citizens. Many of them were passionately patriotic Germans, Poles, Hungarians, and so on. Most of them didn't know or didn't want to know they were Jewish. The Holocaust did not find a unified people, committed to its national or religious heritage. The Jews were then undergoing a certain transformation, they were in the process of assimilation. Suddenly came someone who pointed his finger at them and told them that they carry in their genes something Jewish. My family was not different

You can get a glimpse of it in The Pupil of The Eye. In
many ways the Holocaust returned me to my people, to my
roots. You can see it in my writing. My search for the
right words and sentence structure is a search for my
roots. Through the process of writing I am reconstructing
my heritage, of which I knew nothing before the war broke
out.

E. F. The pattern of persecution and escape underlies many
of your stories about Jews, and it seems to indicate your
conception of Jewish history. What does Judaism, or
Jewish history, mean to you as a positive phenomenon, not
as something defined by external pressures?

A. A. This is a question I wrestle with belletristically, not
conceptually. But if you insist, I will say this--a person
should absorb as much as he can, not only from his own
personal source, but from his tribe as well. The individual
is after all connected to his parents, family and tribe, and
the stronger his ties with them, the richer he becomes.
This involves beliefs, legends, superstitions, etc., and I
am trying to advance in this direction.

E. F. What about your religious roots?

A. A. This is a difficult question. My first life scenes
showed me murder, violence, hostility, ruthlessness. My
childhood memories are an ongoing series of horror
pictures--sadism, on the one hand, and helplessness on
the other. This makes it difficult to accept religion, or
belief in God, in its innocent sense. The world I saw
seemed to be a chaotic arena ruled by blind fate. I could
not, and still cannot, conceive of a benevolent, merciful
God, who is also omniscient, omnipotent, and omni-
present. I don't think that any Holocaust survivor can free
himself of the impression that the world is essentially
dominated by an arbitrary and merciless force. On the

other hand, these people see their own survival as a meaningful fact. This meaning bothers them. How should they construe it with the rest of the evidence? There are several directions to choose from. One possibility is to return to the sources, mainly in order to rediscover the echoes of one's beginnings, in order to listen to the whispers of his roots. I see myself as a man who is searching for meaning in life. This is rather different from being a staunch believer in something. A believer is someone who senses a consciousness, or a direction, and believes in it. The one who searches for meaning has not found the direction yet. I am looking for my roots in the Jewish heritage. But in a sense, I am afraid these roots are lost forever.

E. F. Do you expect your newly translated book, Like The Pupil of The Eye to have a special meaning for the American reader?

A.A. This is a semi-autobiographical novella. I tell of our life in the village with our German neighbors. As I said before, we were not very conscious of our Jewishness. I hate to draw comparisons and I don't want to hint at anything, but since you asked me, I will tell you that there is a similar displacement from one's roots in America. I visited the United States a few years ago. My impression is that Judaism in America is undergoing a constant erosion. The process of assimilation continues despite sporadic outbursts of religious enthusiasm. I see no future for Jews, as Jews, in America. You know, for the first time, we were given a certain chance, a chance, here, in Israel --a rare and precious opportunity to realize ourselves as Jews, without having to be afraid, or to apologize for it. I hope we don't lose this chance. It might never come again. I think that in Israel one can experience and realize his Jewishness more fully than anywhere else. At the same time, things are not so clear-cut in Israel. I am not interested in collectives, but in individuals. But

60

please, I don't want to speak categorically. I know there are many Jews there who desire to live here, and things don't work always the way we want them to. I told you, I am not a preacher. I am afraid of big words. I can only work with the small ones. I am a craftsman of self-effacing words, the hiding, the shy words. I hope the American reader can find them, and perhaps take some of them along with him.

E. F.   How do you judge your own work?

A. A.   I don't have objective criteria with which to judge my own work, if this is what you mean. I don't think of "new criticism" or "old criticism" when I write. The only criterion is the work itself. I don't think there is an author who takes such factors into consideration. His foremost allegiance is to the work itself. One makes an effort to do justice to the work. Its sophistication depends on the level of intelligence or talent of the specific artist.

E. F.   How do you treat critical reviews of your works?

A. A.   If I see that the critic deals with the work itself, that he is well acquainted with what I wrote, I listen to him just as I would to a friend. But if I realize that the critic imposes external criteria or his own predilections on the text, then I'm not interested in what he has to say.

E. F.   I recently read a critical review which claimed that Amos Oz, A. B. Yehoshua and you tend to repeat yourselves in your latest works, that you imitate your own styles and exploit it as sheer mannerisms.

A. A.   What does it mean to repeat oneself? Every true writer deals with two or three motifs throughout his literary career. He tries to develop them, perfect them, examine and re-examine their different aspects, and every new work

61

offers new insight into the same motifs. Take Chagall or Picasso, for example--don't they repeat the same motifs over and over again? I take this kind of criticism as a compliment. When I read a writer who offers me something totally different in every one of his books I become suspicious. Can he be authentic? Where did he gain so much knowledge and experience?

E.F. You started with short stories. Your later works, The Skin and The Garment, Like The Pupil of The Eye, and Years and Hours are novellas. Why do you prefer the longer narrative form?

A.A. I am moving towards a greater fullness of experience. It seems to me that in the novella one can catch the thread in a different length, and perhaps in a way which may disclose more about its nature.

E.F. Do you consider yourself part of a certain Israeli literary milieu?

A.A. To a certain extent, I do. But one must bear in mind that everyone of us has a different biography and a different background. I am different from those authors who continue an indigenous literary tradition. I was a very close friend of Agnon, though I was much younger than he. I see myself perhaps as a pupil, a disciple, but my fundamental experience is different. His work grew out of a solid cultural and literary tradition. I came from a destroyed world.

E.F. What about European influences?

A.A. I would say that the Austro-German writers influenced me most, in terms of literary expression.

E.F. Can you be specific?

A.A.   Kafka and his circle, for example.

E.F.   This is the time for the inevitable technical question. Do you write daily, or wait for the blessed hour of inspiration?

A.A.   I write every day, for many hours. I write and rewrite, until I calm down.

E.F.   Is there anything you'd like to tell me at the end of our interview?

A.A.   There is something paradoxical in this interview. It is meant for an American public, yet I doubt that many Americans read my stories. As I told you, few of my works have been translated. My work consists of nuances. It is hard to translate. It requires reading and listening, very strenuous listening, because it contains whispers, screams which turned into whispers.

AA

AHARON MEGGED

Megged was born in Wloclawcek, Poland in 1920, and emigrated to Israel with his family in 1926. He studied at Herzeliah High School in Tel Aviv, and in 1937 moved to the pioneer training group at Givat-Brener. He was a member of Kibbutz Sdot-Yam from 1938 to 1950. During this time, in 1946, he was sent to the United States and Canada for two years as a representative of "The Young Pioneer." From 1952-1955, Megged was editor-in-chief of Massa (a bi-weekly newspaper) and from 1955 to 1968, he was the editor of Lamerhav (a daily newspaper). He served as cultural attache of the Israeli embassy in London from 1968 to 1971. His works have been translated into English, French, Italian, German and Yiddish, and he has won several literary prizes, among them the Ussishkin Prize for 1955 and 1966, the Brenner Prize for 1957, the Shlonsky Prize for 1963, the Bialik Prize for 1973, and the Fichman Prize for 1973.

Megged has been a regular contributor to Davar since 1971, and in all ways is a prolific writer. A selective list of his publications includes: Mikre ha-kesil, 1960 (Fortunes of A Fool, 1962); Ha-hai al ha-met, 1965 (The Living on The Dead, 1970); Ha-Haim haketsarim, 1972 (The Short Life, 1980); ha-Atalef (The Bat), 1975; Heints u-veno ve-harvah hara'ah (Heints, His Son and The Evil Spirit), 1976; Asahel, 1979 (Asahel, 1982); and Masa be-av (A Voyage in The Month of Av), 1980. The short story, "The Name," is included in Joel Blocker's edition of Israeli Stories, 1962.

BY TRIAL and ERROR

An Interview with Aharon Megged*

E. F. Aharon Megged is a name which is associated in
critical circles with the Palmach generation of the late
forties and early fifties. What do you feel about it?

A. M. I object. I vehemently object to the classification,
mainly because of the preconceived notions it perpetuates.
The pervasive stereotype of the idealistic-nationalistic
Palmach literature is false. It's a myth, it is simply a
myth that the Palmach generation presented the character
of the Sabra as undaunted and flawless hero. You may indeed find such heroes in certain works, but to extend it
over a whole generation is an outrageous generalization.
After all, what is the Palmach literature? It was created
by writers such as Shlomo Nitzan, Tabib, Nissim Aloni,
David Shachar, Benjamin Tamuz. Do they write about
such characters? Look at my characters--none of them
is a hero. They are outsiders, rootless, alienated from
the social and national establishment, they are drifting
and vulnerable! Really, I don't understand the reason for
such rigid formulas. Sure, there are a few stories by Natan
Schacham, and Shamir's <u>With His Own Hands</u>, but these
are exceptions which prove the rule. It's ridiculous to
define beginning writers, most of them in their twenties,
as a cohesive literary wave. Since the 1940s, most of

* *Originally conducted in Hebrew, Tel Aviv, August, 1981.

them changed and developed. Their concepts, their writing, their styles, each took his own direction. Why lock one up for life because of a few youthful errors? Why be consigned to a procrustean bed, penalized by insensitive critics? This is a terrible injustice. I'm not denying the fact that an important transition took place in the early sixties, but the Palmach generation is part of this transition, perhaps with the exception of S. Yizhar, who did not continue writing.

E.F. How would you define the transition from the fifties to the sixties?

A.M. I think we can see it as a growing tendency towards surrealism, maybe escapism. In 1960, I wrote The Case of The Fool. In 1962--The Escape. A.B. Yehoshua, who is identified with the "new wave" published his first book, The Death of The Old Man, in 1962. You see, we all tried to rebel against the Palmach ethos of social solidarity and patriotism in our writing. One of the differences between us and the younger authors of the "new wave" is that we were part of the youth movement. We went on to the Labor Movement, and then joined the Palmach. Most of the younger authors were university students and studied literature, but as I said, the change occurred everywhere.

E.F. In The Short Life (1973), and The Living On The Dead (1974) you return to a realistic mode of writing. Why?

A.M. My earlier realism was closer to naturalism. I think the temporary switch to surrealism was necessary as a phase. From the surrealistic phase I finally arrived at my present mode of realism. All these changes are related, to a great extent, to my personal growth, to events in my own life.

E.F. In The Short Life, there is a quote from the research work of Dr. Elisheva Tal, to the effect that the realistic novel is passe. I understand that this is an ironic quotation. Are you trying to satirize a certain critical bias against realism?

A. M. Of course I object to the notion that realism is dead. I have a pluralistic approach to it all. I think all genres are valid and should coexist side by side. I judge by my own attraction to literary works. I love Kafka and Borges, but I love Bellow and Malamud, for example. I don't believe in fashion in the arts. A work should be judged by its value, not by its genre.

E. F. Whom do you particularly admire in Hebrew literature?

A. M. Agnon, Brenner, the early Hazar.

E. F. Are you aware of their influence on your work?

A. M. Oh, yes. In my youth I tried to imitate Agnon and Hazar. But I think I was mainly influenced by foreign literature, in so far as I know. Above all, I think Gogol had a tremendous impact on me.

E. F. Many of your protagonists, for example, Rieger in The Bat (1975) or Ruby, in Heinz, His Son and the Evil Spirit (1979) are not only uprooted but outright insane. Is this portrayal of alienation part of the socio-cultural atmosphere we discussed above?

A. M. Most of my characters are projections of certain aspects of my own psyche. They grow out of my personal experiences. I write about outsiders because I can understand them and identify with them. I could never write about the protagonist of With His Own Hands, for example, a heroic, well integrated and admirable character. This is exactly the plot of the Living on The Dead, a man who tries to write about a hero and fails. Like the narrator, Yonas, I too would fail if I had to describe a hero. Some

67

people say that, in this novel, I create and destroy an idol.
But it's not that simple. Davidov is heroic as a Halutz.
He is an idealist, always loyal to the Zionist cause. In
this sense he remains a hero. But in his personal life he
is not so loyal, and he is not exactly a hero. His weak-
nesses as a family man, however, don't have to eclipse
his positive traits as a national hero. Let me give you an
example from the biographies of artists. Balzac, for
example. He was a great artist, but his biographies re-
veal a stingy, greedy, quarrelsome and lascivious man.
Will I therefore admire him less for his art? Nonsense.
There are many other examples. Weakness in a certain
field does not preclude greatness in another.

E.F. It's hard to believe that you identify or empathize
with all your protagonists, especially with a fanatic
nationalist like Rieger.

A.M. You know, I once wrote an article about the writer
as Pygmalion. In the process of creating something
hideous, a symbol to be despised, he falls in love with it.
Gershon Rieger is the dark side of my moon. I can hardly
imagine a character who can better represent my ideological opposite. I guess I wanted to know what it feels
like to be a right wing extremist, and to my great surprise,
I grew to love him. I understood him better. Just like
with real people, the more we understand, the more we
forgive.

E.F. Though the character of the outsider is closely related to your personal life, the drama of alienation is intensely Israeli. Are you perhaps trying to convey through
these alienated characters a message about the "Condition
Israelienne?"

A.M. Consciously, I am not trying to convey a message
or a prophecy. What makes me write is a wish to create

characters, and make them alive. There is often a certain character which asks to be created, it bursts out of me. When I feel it's ready, I start writing. It is this character that creates its social context, its relations with other characters, and so on. In my works, the socio-political context is usually Israeli. This is perhaps where I differ from the younger generation, the writers in their late twenties and early thirties --such as Yotam Hareuveni. At this point comes in the idea or what you call "message." The Zionist message, if you want, enters into the Israeli context which I use for my characters. But the idea is not my primary motivation or goal. It is first and foremost a desire to describe a human predicament.

E. F. Viewed chronologically, your works seem to portray an ever increasing alienation from the Zionist idea or Israeli raison d'être. The gap between the kibbutz idealism and the city materialism in Hedvah and I (1955) is innocuous compared to the radical break from society in your last novel, A Voyage In the Month of Ab (1980). How would you explain it?

A. M. Now that you mention it, I think you're right. There is a growing alienation, a growing distance from the collective. I guess the cracks are becoming more and more visible. The problems are getting closer to the roots of Zionism. At that time, the conviction was stronger, purer and more innocent. The situation is much more complex now. What we took for granted became rather questionable, and increasingly problematic.

E. F. In Asahel (1978) you coined many interesting neologisms. Is the need to create language in addition to literature a welcome task?

A. M. That depends on what one is trying to write. Many authors managed to create a personal Hebrew. Amalia

Carmon writes in a language all her own. So does Appelfeld. Their characters are comfortable with this personal
language. But in a realistic novel, where one's goal is to
reproduce an Israeli context, a "tranche de vie," everyday
dialogue and natural fluent speech, one faces a problem,
because Hebrew in reality is not yet natural and fluent.
People still struggle with the right words, the right expressions. Even native speakers are still uneasy about right
and wrong. Although I'm not myself a native--I was born
in Poland--Hebrew is my mother tongue. Both my parents
spoke Hebrew at home. It's our natural language, but we
don't quite feel at ease with it. In English, for example,
people use set patterns like well worn clothes. Hebrew is
not yet used enough to serve as a natural way of expression.
When I say something, I feel I say it for the first time.
When I write, I have to construct the sentence from the
beginning--words, syntax, grammar--all. In many cases
I use the Bible and other classical sources for help. This
is a blessing in disguise, because it forces us to interact
closely with our classical sources. In so far as the problem
is concerned--it will be solved in time. Only time will make
us fluent and at ease with our own reborn language.

E.F. What are your own favorite works, including the
occasional plays you wrote?

A.M. Frankly, I don't like my plays very much. I think I
wrote them far too fast. I didn't take them seriously
enough. I'm not terribly pleased with my earlier works,
such as Hedvah and I, and Israel-Brothers. They seem to
be beginner's works. I do like The Notebooks of Evyatar,
Asahel, and Heinz His Son and The Evil Spirit. I wouldn't
write Hevdah and I now, but the only way to have realized
it was by trying it out. One doesn't grow without trial and
error. The most important thing is to keep working, and
never stand still.

AM

YORAM KANIUK

Yoram Kaniuk was born in Tel Aviv in 1930. During
the 1948 war he served in the Palmach (the pre-state
military forces), and was wounded in the battle of Jerusalem. He studied painting in Paris and continued his education in the United States. He started his career as a painter,
and later worked as a theater and film critic for the news-
papers, Davar and Lamerhave. At present, he continues
to be a regular contributor to the cultural supplement,
Devar Hashavua.

Kaniuk's works were translated into numerous languages
and have been published in the United States, as well as in
England, Italy, France, Finland, Sweden, Portugal, Brazil
and Denmark. Among his publications are Ha-yored
lemala, 1963 (The Acrophile, 1961); Himmo melekh
yerushalaim, 1966 (Himmo, King of Jerusalem, 1969);
Adam ben kelev, 1969 (Adam Resurrected, 1971); Susets,
1973 (Rocking Horse, 1977); Ha-sipur al doda shlomtsion
ha-gedola, 1975 (The Story of Aunt Shlomzion the Great,
1979); Ha-yehudi ha-aharon (The Last Jew), 1982.
"Parched Earth" appeared in Joel Blocker's edition of
Israeli Stories, 1962.

Israeli Literature And The Spectre of Jewish History

An Interview with Yoram Kaniuk
(Tel Aviv, August, 1981)

E. F. What is your last novel, The Last Jew, about?

Y. K. The Last Jew spans the history of a family over several generations, unfolding simultaneously in Europe and in Israel. The protagonist is a native Israeli, who becomes embroiled in the Holocaust, while in search of his father. Finally he manages to escape because he possesses certain information. The point is the precariousness of Jewish life, in Israel or in Europe. The point is that we all survived by coincidence. There is a paradox in the existence of the state of Israel. Our political sovereignty was granted to us by nations who at a certain moment in history felt regret for what they had done to the Jews. But the Jews for whom Israel was to compensate are no longer alive. The price we had to pay was too high. The situation is similar to the story of the Ten Martyrs tortured by the Romans. I think their saying about the Messiah, "He should come, but I should not see him," applies to our life here. If the price of redemption is so high, it's better not to be redeemed at all. The reality of redemption loses its meaning.

This problem has plagued me for a very long time. I think that among the native Israeli writers, Haim Guri and I are the only ones who deal with this problem so extensively.

E. F. What about Hanoch Bartov?

Y. K. Bartov wrote about the subject, and so did Yehuda

Amichai, for example. But it is not a central problem in
their literary world. I am talking about the tension between
the Jew and the Israeli, the "here" and "there." Amos Oz
and A.B. Yehoshua, or Amalia Kahana-Carmon are not
interested in the Jewish problem.

E.F. Does "there" include the United States as well as
Europe?

Y.K. The United States does not interest me that much.
I spent ten years in America, and these were important
for my growth and development, but in my literary world,
America is marginal.

E.F. It serves as background in The Acrophile and in
Rocking Horse.

Y.K. In Rocking Horse I needed a beginning for a plot
which takes place in Israel. I use America for my short
pieces. I assume that it interests me, in so far as it
represents part of the Jewish dilemma.

E.F. What is the Jewish dilemma?

Y.K. I am talking about the relationship between "Jew"
and "Israeli." Who am I? What is my identity in essence?
The dilemma involves the diaspora, anti-Semitism, the
kind of country I want to live in, religion. Despite my
notorious objection to the religious establishment, I read
Ein Ya'akov and the Zohar. I studied the Zohar long before
it became fashionable, as early as 1949. At the same
time I identified with the Canaanites, who rejected Judaism
completely.* My schizophrenia was evident from a very
early stage in my life.

*
Mainly a literary movement, which made use of Canaanite
mythology. The poet, Yonatan Ratosh, was a leading exponent.

73

E. F.   How would you compare The Last Jew to your previous work?

Y.K.   I think that all my life, in all my works, I had tried
to write The Last Jew. I started to write the novel in 1963.
In the meantime I wrote Adam Resurrected, Rocking Horse
and Aunt Shlomzion the Great, but all this time I kept turning to the novel and leaving it. After I completed Aunt
Shlomzion in 1974, I returned to The Last Jew and worked
on it till 1981. I think that in many ways this novel contains all the themes I deal with in my other works--the
War of Independence, the Holocaust, the absurdity of
Jewish history, the dilemma of the Jewish people, the predicament of the state of Israel, the relationship between Jew
and Israeli. In The Last Jew I completed a cycle. I finally
said what I wanted to say. I don't know what I'll do next,
but I do know that at this point, I reached the end of a long
struggle.

E. F.   As a native Israeli who did not experience the Holocaust, have you felt at times that your personal background
was not adequate for describing the life of a survivor in
Israel?

Y.K.   Originally I was a painter. I started to write because
I felt I had a testimony to give. As a native Israeli I had
very little in common with European Jews. Like many
others, I was taught to reject the Diaspora. After the War
of Independence, I worked aboard a refugee ship. This was
after I had been wounded in battle, and after I had witnessed
how cruel human beings can be to each other, and how senseless and wasteful war is. Years later I wrote "The Vultures"
against this background. Nevertheless, my encounter with
the refugees was by far the most traumatic event I have
experienced. Europe was still ravaged, and the refugees
had arrived from transitory camps in Italy. From that
point on the Holocaust became an obsession for me. I knew

I could easily have been one of them. The feeling that it could have happened to me, and that perhaps it should have happened to me, that I was spared by sheer coincidence, became the dominant thing in my life. I spent four years thinking myself to be a holocaust survivor. I met more refugees and read whatever I could. I experienced a kind of déja vu, a feeling that I was there myself. When Israel accepted reparation money from Germany, I was in the United States, and I refused to return because I did not want to live in the houses and use the roads built with German money.

I don't know whether I succeeded in conveying what I had to convey. I think I came fairly close in Adam Resurrected. Many survivors who read the book told me that it brought back memories and revived scenes they had seen. People who read parts of The Last Jew told me the same thing. If literature gives legitimacy to the absurd, my writing legitimatizes the absurd of conveying something I did not experience physically.

E.F. Adam Resurrected was received enthusiastically by American critics, such as Susan Sontag. In Israel, the reviews were more reserved. How do you explain this?

Y.K. The book got very good reviews in France, and especially in Sweden and Denmark. Critics told me that the critical enthusiasm could only compare with A Hundred Years of Solitude. It got a good response in the United States when it was first published there in English, and then it was rediscovered by Susan Sontag and Arthur Miller. Sontag considered it one of the most important books of the last fifty years. It also got very good reviews in Holland, and it is soon to be published in Iceland, Brazil, and in Portugal. In Israel, however, when it came out, in 1968, the critical response was rather reserved. Four reviews in all dealt with the book. The problem is that Israeli critics judge literature strictly in terms of the local scene.

When they deal with Hebrew writers, they completely ignore other literatures. They discuss the influence of Berdichevsky on Amos Oz, and that of Agnon on A. B. Yehoshua, and remain oblivious to the effect of foreign literatures on their works. Literature is undoubtedly a product of a national culture. At the same time, however, it is inspired by other national cultures. Hebrew literature does not exist in a vacuum. It is part of a wider frame of reference--of world literature. An Israeli contemporary writer need not be influenced only by Brenner. He could be influenced, even to a greater degree, by Thomas Mann. Mann, for example, definitely influenced Agnon, and Kafka did too, unquestionably. Agnon may have denied it, but this doesn't change the fact. Faulkner influenced French and Latin American authors. Literature in other countries is examined in terms of genres, themes, etc. In Hebrew literature everything is categorized into generations--the generation of the Palmach, of the State, etc.

E. F.   Can you classify your own work in any of these categories?

Y. K.   That's precisely the point. My work does not belong to the Palmach, and not quite to the State's generation. It contains elements of both trends, and probably European and American influences. When a writer defies the critics' preconceived notions and classifications, he is doomed. Recently a book on contemporary Hebrew literature was published in Denmark, and was severely criticized for not mentioning my work. The writer apologized, saying that she simply did not know how to classify me, and since she used literary generations as her basic pattern of analysis, there was no place for me. The same confusion surrounded Adam Resurrected in Israel. Is it "holocaust literature?" Yes and no. Is it realistic or fantastic? Both. Is it comic or tragic? Both. What do you do in this case? The safest thing is not to discuss it. The critics here are also obsessed by questions of forms and aesthetics, and it seems to me that Agnon was rather destructive in this regard. I am not a fan of allusions and allegories, on which Israeli critics spend so much time. I prefer Brenner's directness and Berdichevsky's frank writing, to the symbolic convolutions of Agnon.

E.F. In some of your works the plot progression implies an ideological message. In Rocking Horse, for instance, the protagonist returns to himself by traveling back to Israel. Is the message intentional?

Y.K. I restrict my ideologies to my political essays. In fiction I belong to the school of authors who are tale spinners. I like to tell stories. I have noticed, however, that whereas in my political thinking I am a liberal and a socialist, in my literary writing I am a reactionary who believes in blood relations, kinship and genealogy. In my stories I believe in mysterious links between relatives, who are separated by geographical distance and historical generations. It seems to me that my characters should be asked about me, and not vice versa. In essence I see myself as a writer of characters rather than of plots. From this point of view, I am closer to the nineteenth century literature than to contemporary literature. If you take, for example, A Hundred Years of Solitude, it's a great story, but you won't find in it characters like Madame Bovary or Piere Bazuchov. In the nineteenth century, the story was spinned out of the character. In my writing too, the character is the center of the story. My character is greater than life. Most of the characters in contemporary Israeli fiction are anti-heroes. In Agnon, Brenner, and Yehoshua, for example, the heroes are ordinary people, perhaps too ordinary. I am not evaluating or criticizing, I am only trying to point out differences. The characters of Adam, of Shlomzion, are greater than life. They dictate the story, they determine the progression of the plot. Now this is an additional problem. It took the Israeli critics a long time to realize that I am an author of characters. They were looking for a plot or a symbolic constellation in my stories, and naturally didn't find it.

E. F. Many of your characters seem to be on the verge of a nervous breakdown or insanity. What is behind this pattern?

Y. K. I think this stems from the general genre which I employ, the grotesque. My characters are exaggerated. This reminds me of a recent conversation with Haim Shoham from Bar-Ilan University, who told me that in his second reading of Adam Resurrected, he laughed. He didn't laugh ten years ago, when he read it for the first time. But most readers here missed the humor, unlike the Americans, who perceived it immediately. Perhaps this was because they are more tuned in to the unique quality of Jewish humor, which is, to a large extent, black humor, laughing at the absurdity and grotesquery of life. One of the peculiar things about contemporary Israeli literature is the lack of humor. I am not talking about comedians, like Ephraim Kishon or Dan Ben-Amotz. Now, people may laugh when they feel the context is right. But in novels about the Holocaust, they don't know how to relate to it. They are afraid to laugh.

One way to confront the Jewish or Israeli reality is to tear out one's hair and howl, following Brenner's "nevertheless" and "beyond despair." The other way is to laugh, laugh at the insanity of it all. The Jews have known it for many generations. The Israelis have only recently begun to realize that a viable attitude to their national history must include humor.

Now, in my grotesques, I try to combine horror and laughter. My characters are insane because I feel a deep attraction to insanity. The only thing which holds my demons down is my writing. I believe--and this is the reactionary in me--that I carry genes of my Frankist fore-fathers.*My family comes from the Ukraine, the birth-place of the movement. I know this insanity well. I carry it in me. In The Last Jew, I combined all these legends, the tales of absurdity, humor and despair, Hasidism, Frankism, Zionism.

E. F. You see Zionism as a form of madness? Another episode in a history of instabilities and calamities?

Y. K. I don't know. The first two Hebrew kingdoms were destroyed, the third may also be destroyed. The whole story has lasted--what--a total of one hundred years? It doesn't look too good at the moment. In fact, since 1948 it never seemed to justify optimism. I don't know whether Israel will be an episode, or whether it will continue to exist. I only think that those who believe that we can sever our ties with the Jewish story are wrong. They are wrong because, although it's important to become an integral part of the Near East, it is just as important to remember that Zionism is part and parcel of Judaism, and that al-though it rebelled against Jewish tradition, it carries it on in a very deep and real sense, not necessarily in a religious sense.

I don't think that the law preserved the Jews, I think the Jews preserved the Jewish law. I think that Judaism is not merely a religion, it's far more complex and inclusive. In-sofar as Israel is concerned, I am fascinated by what has happened here. I wrote about it quite a bit in Rocking Horse, Aunt Shlomzion, and other places. I wrote perhaps with irony, but all things considered, one can't help being ironic about the Zionist adventure--Jews rise up, stop their history and rebuild their state in the middle of the world, in the midst of history, just like that. There's something funny

* A splinter sect, in the 18th cent., of a larger messianic movement. Its founder, Jacob Frank, believed himself to be an incarnation of God.

in it, funny and sad at the same time. There's something
very Jewish about it too. In its absurdity, Zionism continues the Jewish insanity, which had always been there,
in different forms and different names. It was called
Kabbala, Frankism, Hasidism, and now it's Zionism. The
edge of this insanity was somewhat blunted by the historians
who found it necessary to neutralize it by classifying and
tabulating it. So, even if it turns out to be a historical
episode, it will be one of the most representative and characteristic episodes of Jewish history.

E.F. I find that several of your works, such as "The
Parched Earth" are rather nostalgic.

Y.K. "The Parched Earth" was my first story. I wrote
it during my long visit to the United States. I missed
Israel bitterly at that time. I remembered the small community of Tel Aviv, the clean swept streets on Friday eve-
ning, everyone dressed in white, Mr. Abarbanel greeting
my father from a distance, the clear sea, the camel
caravans, the sycamores, the Sabras. I missed the golden
sand dunes on the beach, the concerts of the Philharmonic
Orchestra, the salad and the yogurt, the simplicity and
tranquility of those antediluvian days.
    Of course there were others, such as the family of Aunt
Shlomzion, who dealt with stocks and bonds and tried to get
rich quickly. On the whole, however, a rather unique and
cohesive society developed in Palestine. I missed it. Even
now I sometimes do. And I know I am not the only one. At
the same time, we must remember that, while we were
enjoying the Philharmonic Orchestra, millions of Jews were
slaughtered in Europe. So to be totally nostalgic about "those
days" is naive and provincial, though nostalgia may penetrate our writings imperceptibly now and then. Is there a
Hebrew writer who lived in Palestine in the 1930s and 40s
who can avoid it, who doesn't miss his childhood?

E. F. Notwithstanding your interest in the Jewish dilemma, some of your major works deal with typically Israeli themes, such as the gap between the Zionist and the socio-political reality. This is especially obtrusive in Himmo, King of Jerusalem, Rocking Horse, and even in Adam Resurrected.

Y.K. The theme of disillusionment runs throughout my political essays, and I am sure it exists in my fiction as well. But I am not so sure that this is the right definition. Personally I haven't experienced a great disappointment, because I haven't had a chance to delude myself for long. I was very young when the War of Independence broke out. At the same time, I was old enough to perceive the problems which existed even before the establishment of the State, unlike the younger authors who tend to idealize that period. I guess the sense of disillusionment is more collective than personal. The reality which was established is not what my grandfather and yours dreamed about and longed for. The society which was created here is not the one that the Zionist thinkers had contemplated. But the gap between the ideal and the reality is almost inevitable in human history. We always search for the face we had had before we were born.

E. F. In Himmo, King of Jerusalem and to an extent in the Acrophile you use an objective and--for lack of a better term--a more restrained style. In your later work, your style tends to be more expansive and less controlled. You seem to give your protagonist full rein with his internal monologues and associations. Are you aware of this change ?

Y.K. I found that this was my most natural voice. I talk and think this way, even in my letters I use this style.

E. F. What is the story behind Himmo, King of Jerusalem?

Y.K. Himmo is based on a personal experience. During
the war of 1948 I was hospitalized in an Italian monastery
in Jerusalem, and beside me was a dying soldier just like
Himmo. I wanted to forget it, but I had to tell the story.
Some people think I intended to convey a message about
the horrors of the war and the need to put an end to it. But
messages are irrelevant.

E.F. You don't believe that art can change reality?

Y.K. The commander of Auschwitz read the best of European literature, and listened to the best classical music.
Did that make him more human? Which work of art ever
changed the world?---But that's what I was trying to do
in Rocking Horse. I wanted to explain why we, the generation which was raised to believe in liberalism, socialism
and humanism, why we are in fact crazy--because we
actually believed that ideas and art can change the world.
Did "Guernica" or the paintings of Goya stop the wars?
Did War and Peace make the world better? Art doesn't
change reality. It may only affect an individual reader for
a while. Literature is, after all, legends which are the
products of our demons. How can legends change facts?
Literature is an exercise in exorcising demons. I am
writing because I want to get rid of my demons, or at least
control them. In the final analysis, literature is made up
of myth. It is too fragile for reality. I think that every
author, deep in his heart, wants to be a prophet, but even
the prophets didn't change anything. They were considered
half wits, they were ridiculed by the public and persecuted
by kings. Only later, after the expulsion from Canaan, did
the people understand that Jeremiah and Elijah were more
important than Ahab. So in the canon they allotted two
chapters to the king and a whole book to the prophet. But
the contemporaries of the prophets considered them to be
traitors and persecuted them whenever they could. Who
were the prophets, after all? They were the poets of antiquity.

E.F. The comparison between a poet and a prophet is
quite common in modern Hebrew literature. Do you think
of yourself as a spiritual leader?

Y.K. I have given this question considerable thought. In
the past, Hebrew authors enjoyed a unique status. They
were considered not only artists, but also perhaps mainly
as men of the spirit. Writers were influential because the
country was rebuilt by idealists who were also pragmatic.
The second Aliya* created the rare combination of spirit
and action. The authors were involved with the actual
process of growth. And the political leaders were artists
too--Berl Katzenelsohn, Agnon, Asher Barash, and later,
Alterman. David Ben-Gurion used to say that when he
wanted to listen to his conscience, he read Alterman. And
I don't know whether this is good or bad. In Europe,
literature is still an event worthy of news coverage. Authors
in Sweden and Denmark are much more respected than here,
though we have a larger readership. Israel seems to follow
the American example, I think, where the author is a kind
of clown, unless he publishes a best seller and becomes
rich.

E.F. Despite your focus on the Jewish-Israeli experience
your work has been widely translated. How do you explain
the interest of non-Jewish readers in your work?

Y.K. The more specific and local a story is, the more
interesting it is for the outside reader. Stories about
threesomes mating with foursomes in the most spectacular
patterns--such stories exist everywhere. But a story
about a couple who survived the Holocaust, each partner
having lost their children, and they come to Israel and
create a new family, but lose their first son in war and
their second daughter in an automobile accident--this

*wave of Jewish immigrants into Israel

83

situation can be found only here. Or a situation in which immigrants flock together to find refuge in Israel, after years of pogroms and persecution, and find out that they must confront new enemies who hate them for different reasons, and survive not only war but many wars, because the conflict is open ended and cannot be settled. The sensation that one lives under eighty meters of fodder all the time, that one lives in the intersection of nightmares and picnics--you survive a nightmare and later have a picnic. Seizing the day, living quickly, going on trips and having barbecues, knowing all the time that any day, any minute, something awful may explode and put an end to the celebration--this nervous energy of instant entertainment between battles--this is Israel. On a certain level, this situation exists everywhere, and therefore a reader in France or Sweden can identify with it. At the same time, such a story presents a familiar reality, in a more extreme way. This Israeli story epitomizes life everywhere, under the constant threat of the atomic bomb, for example. Nevertheless, it's different, it's unique. That's why <u>Adam Resurrected</u> appealed to so many foreign readers, and I didn't need to look far and wide for my basic plot. It was available here in this country, whose everyday life challenges the most contrived drama and the most sophisticated imagination.

E.F. Do you feel that your translated work loses much of its original impact?

Y.K. In a sense I do, but in many ways I think it gains something in translation. When I write in Hebrew, I may be lured by the sound or feeling of certain words. When I read my work in translation, I see it as it is, naked, with no alluring clothes or appealing ornaments. It forces me to come closer to the things I want to touch and the ideas I want to convey. On the other hand, certain things can never be translated. Every word in Hebrew has a history. The simplest day-to-day vocabulary evokes Biblical or Talmudic connotations. In a foreign language, the double perspective of the pedestrian and the sublime is bound to be lost.

YEHUDA AMICHAI

Yehuda Amichai was born in Wurtzburg, Germany and emigrated to Israel in 1936 at the age of twelve. He studied at the "Ma'aleh" High School in Jerusalem, and later graduated from Hebrew University, and is presently teaching Hebrew literature at the Haim Greenberg College in Jerusalem. He has participated in several international poetry festivals--in Spoletto, London, Rotterdam, and Washington, and has been a visiting lecturer in the United States. He has also won several literature awards--in 1975, the Bialik Award for Literature, and in 1981, the distinguished Israel Prize.

Many of Amichai's poems have been translated into English and his work is well known to poetry readers in the United States. His numerous volumes include, among others, Be-merhak shtei tikvot (At A Distance of Two Hopes), 1958; Shirim 1948-1962 (Poems 1948-1962) 1962; Akhshav ba-ra'ash (Now In This Noise), 1969; Selected Poems, 1968; Poems from Songs of Jerusalem and Myself, 1973; Ha-zeman, 1977 (Time, 1979); Amen, 1978; Love Poems (a bilingual edition), 1981.

His fictional works include: Ba-ruah hanora'a ha-zot (In This Terrible Wind), 1961; Lo mikan lo me-akhshav, 1963 (Not of This Time, Not of This Place, 1968); Mi yitneni malon, 1972 (Travels of A Latter Day Benjamin of Tudela, 1976). Amichai's "Battle For The Hill" appeared in Joel Blocker's edition of Israeli Stories, 1962; and "The Times My Father Died" is included in Robert Alter's edition of Modern Hebrew Literature, 1975.

"I AM A MAN WHO WRITES POEMS"

Interview with Yehuda Amichai*

E.F. What do you feel about the Israel Prize Poetry
award which you recently won?

Y.A. I felt very good about it, but I don't see it as an
apotheosis or a victory of any sort. With or without a
prize I would go on writing. I never write for the effect
my poetry may or may not produce. I write because it
makes me feel good. Poetry for me is a release, because
it helps me locate my pain and transform it into words.
You know my poem, "My Son My Son, My Head My Head?"
It is my instinctive way of touching a wound. It also organ-
izes the world for me. It puts some order into the ongoing
chaos. It gives me something to hold on to, "meaning,"
if you like. The desire to share it with others, or to be
loved and appreciated for it comes later. The reward is
by no means a part of the creative process.

E.F. What is the creative process? How is your poem
born?

Y.A. First comes the desire to translate my feelings into
words. Whenever I feel love or pain, I look around me
and search for the available materials which can help me

* Interview was conducted in Hebrew: Austin, Texas,
March 22, 1982.

express my feelings. I measure my sensibilities against
the objects which I find around me. Children do it all the
time. You hear them say, "I love you, like the sky, like
the sun." The impulse to compare your inner world to the
world around you is very natural, and this is how a metaphor
is born. The basic thing is to establish a contact between
time, space and words. The right metaphor is the core of
my poem. I don't want to create the impression that the
metaphors flow out of me right onto the paper. Despite the
emotional beginning, my mind too is put to work. I select
the metaphors rationally and carefully. The process is not
as spontaneous as it seems. My writing process, on the
other hand, is not as disciplined. I don't follow a regular
routine. An idea or an image may strike me while I walk,
talk, or do something. If I have a piece of paper, I jot it
down. If not, I forget, and sometimes the poem returns to
me after many years. But really, I don't believe in theor-
izing so much about poetry. If you noticed, I never write
poems about poetry. I know there are many poets who
philosophize about it a lot. But then again, I am not a pro-
fessional poet. I don't grow long hair, I don't even smoke
dope. I am a regular person, I also happen to write poems,
and to enjoy it tremendously. I should add that I am also a
very lazy man, or else I would write fiction.

E.F. One of your books bears the title, <u>Now In The Noise.</u>
How does the tumult of Israeli life affect your poetry?

Y.A. The noise is inspiring and at the same time disturbing.
Sometimes, I feel the need to flee, to escape to a quiet and
peaceful place, where I can listen to my own voice. When
you live in Israel, it is impossible to stand by and watch the
scene as an outsider. You must get involved. Shortly after
my family migrated to Palestine, I enlisted in the Brigade,
later in the Palmach, and then I fought in the Israel Defense
Army, like everybody else. Of course at times it seems
that there's too much noise. On the other hand, had my

parents stayed in Germany, I doubt that I would have been able to write anything at all. Had they preferred to go to the United States, I may have become a doctor or a lawyer. Who knows? This noise in Israel may upset me at times, but it also allows me to hear things, and speak with unique voices.

E. F. Despite your personal identification with and participation in the collective struggle your poetic person complains of fatigue and alienation. This is particularly strong in "I Want to Sleep on My Bed." In the story, "Battle For The Hill," war is depicted as a meaningless activity.

Y. A. I started to write in the fifties. We had a chance to wake up from our grand dreams, and unrealistic expectations. Yes, there is a sense of resignation in my poetry, but I think it is very different from the despair you find in some of the contemporary writers. As to the disgust with the war, I think that this characterizes the Israeli attitude to war--you fight for survival with the same passion that you hate the war. Our greatest heroes are those who are most dedicated to peace.

E. F. Resignation is also the attitude which characterizes your love poems. Most of the poems which are addressed to "my girl" refer to extinguished passions.

Y. A. "My girl, " "my child" or "my father" represent for me signposts. They map out my life for me. These persons summarize certain phases in my life, and usually the end of the phase. When I address them, I address a part of myself which is gone. Most of these poetic dialogues refer to intensely personal experiences. They are not empty poses. Most of my love poems refer to bygone experiences because this is the nature of love poetry. When you are in love, you don't reflect on it, analyze or summarize it. You simply experience it. Only when the experience is over, am I able to confront it. That's why I write so much about my father, who died thirty years ago, and so little about my mother who is still alive.

E.F. The persona of your father represents in many poems the Jewish traditional past. In these, as well as in poems addressed to, or revolving around God, there is a strong element of despair.

Y.A. I rebelled against my father. He believed in a traditional Jewish God. He did not approve of my ways. One of the things he could not understand was the fact that it is much harder to be a Jew in Israel than in the Diaspora, because there, one is automatically defined by a different environment, whereas here one must continually redefine his "Jewish" identity. The word "God" in my poems, does not refer to the traditional monotheistic interpretation, but to a universal principle. These poems are usually bitter because this principle, "fate" or "humanity" let me down. Whatever was supposed to be "God" wasn't there when he was most needed. These poems express my personal view of atheism, but in this sense I am not different from many European writers whose poetry is iconoclastic.

E.F. How does the language of the Bible, the holy language, work in your iconoclastic poems?

Y.A. The language does most of my work for me. Every word we use carries in and of itself connotations from the Bible, the Siddur, the Midrash, the Talmud. Every word reverberates through the halls of Jewish history. Coming from a religious background, the spoken language I use still retains for me the original traditional flavor. In my poems I work with both levels, the new and the old, simultaneously. In my poems, I try to recreate and re-interpret. In this sense my writing is genuinely Jewish. In my opinion, Jewish literature consists of the endless interpretations of the source. This is what Rashi did, and this is what modern Zionism did. In this sense, modern Hebrew is really a metaphor for the Zionist endeavor--a reawakening, a revival, which means both change and continuity. What is Zionism if not a reinterpretation of the Biblical verse, "David, King of Jerusalem continues to live?"

E. F. Your novel, Not Of This Place, Not Of This Time, uses a double point of view. The protagonist, Yoel, lives in pre-holocaust Germany and Israel at the same time. What did you intend to convey by this structure?

Y. A. The novel is based on a personal experience. It is a love story. I loved the girl in Germany, during my child-hood, and I loved the American girl I met in Jerusalem. Both symbolize and summarize two different periods in my life. I wanted to be in both places with both girls at the same time. In life one cannot accomplish it. In a novel it is possible to live through different times and places at the same time.

E. F. Why do you prefer to write poetry?

Y. A. As I told you, I am lazy. Novels take a long time to write. In a poem you convey the essence of the thing. Novels fit better in a cold climate, in Russia, Norway, England. In Mediterranean countries poetry is stronger than prose. Israel is not different in this sense. In fact, I think that Israeli poetry is one of the best in the world. It is also widely read. Much more so than in England or in the United States. Hebrew prose, on the other hand, does not fare that well. Perhaps because Hebrew poetry has a long tradition of over three thousand years, whereas Hebrew fiction has only been around for the past two hundred years. Above all, it seems to me that poetry fits the Is-raeli situation better. Our predicament needs a compact, intense and immediate form. Prose fiction requires time and some historical perspective. We haven't been around long enough. We need more time.

E. F. Which poets do you admire most?

Y. A. My favorite European poets are Eliot and Auden. In Hebrew poetry, I think the best are the medieval poets. I admire especially Rabbi Shmuel Hanagid. In modern Hebrew poetry, I admire Lea Goldberg in particular.

E. F. You are cited by literary critics as one of the poets who initiated the new wave in Israeli poetry. Were you aware of your poetic rebellion against the generation of Shlonsky and Alterman?

Y. A. The critical categories, waves, and titles don't mean much to me. They serve critics more than poets. I started writing because I wanted to, because I had something to say, and not because I decided to create a new wave. My poetry was not born as a protest against Shlonsky and Alterman, anymore than I was born as a protest against my own parents. Retroactively, perhaps I introduced something new, but I was not conscious of it at the time.

E. F. You have recently published Questions and Answers in Israel, and Love Poems in the United States. What are you working on at present?

Y. A. I cannot give you the title yet, but it is a very interesting project. I am working on dozens of poems simultaneously. I never did it before. Normally, I complete one poem and continue with the next one. This time I am working on many of them at the same time. It's like painting. You start something, leave it, turn to another detail, then return to the first pattern. It is very exciting.

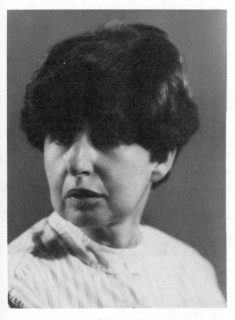

ITAMAR YAOZ-KEST

AMALIA KAHANA-CARMON

S. YIZHAR

GERSHON SHAKED

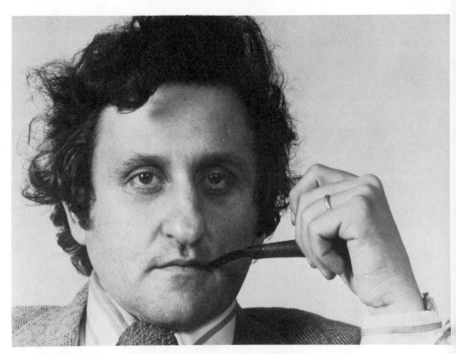

A.B. YEHOSHUA

AHARON APPELFELD

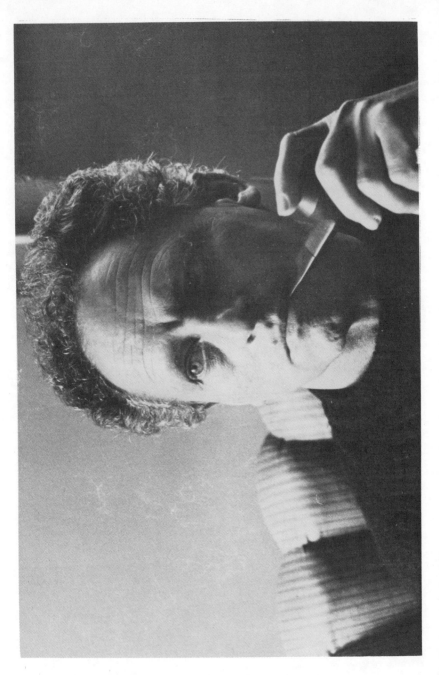

AHARON MEGGED